D1107978

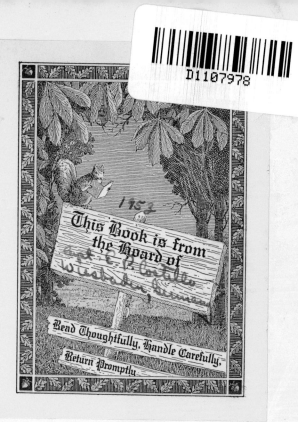

1953

This Book is from
the Hoard of
Capt. C. P. Costello
Wiesbaden, Germany

Read Thoughtfully, Handle Carefully,

Return Promptly

RUSSIA AFTER STALIN

By the same Author

STALIN: *A Political Biography*

RUSSIA
AFTER
STALIN

WITH A POSTSCRIPT ON
THE BERIA AFFAIR

BY

ISAAC DEUTSCHER

HAMISH HAMILTON
LONDON

DK
274
D43

First published in Great Britain, 1953
by Hamish Hamilton Ltd
90 *Great Russell St London WC*1

Second Edition, August 1953

PRINTED IN GREAT BRITAIN
BY WESTERN PRINTING SERVICES LTD, BRISTOL

FOREWORD

THE book I am now placing in the reader's hand has had a curious history. I began writing it in the middle of March 1953, some days after Stalin's death. I intended to sum up broadly the Stalin era and to deduce from the summary a few tentative prognostications. I concluded the introductory chapter with the forecast that a break with the Stalin era was about to begin in Russia. I had made the same forecast in an article written for the *Manchester Guardian* a few hours before Stalin's death. My friends, among them eminent students of Soviet affairs, shook their heads sceptically.

By the time I had concluded the first few chapters startling changes were already occurring in Moscow. Malenkov's government decreed an amnesty and cleared the air of the last, poisonous scandal of the Stalin era, the so-called conspiracy of the Kremlin doctors. I willingly admit that I had not expected that my prognostication would begin to come true so soon. I had thought in terms of months and years, not of days and weeks. This fact accounts for a certain lack of stylistic uniformity in the book. At its beginning I discussed expected developments in the future tense; later I had to describe these developments in the present and even the past tense. I have made no attempt to eliminate these discrepancies. A historian who speeds to the place where past, present, and future meet and tries to describe the scene takes many risks, not only stylistic ones; and he can hardly describe the scene unless he indulges in a certain amount of thinking aloud.

My main purpose, however, has been to offer an inter-

5

42766

pretation of an important historical change, an interpretation based on facts and on an analysis of the basic trends at work in Soviet society. It is primarily in the long perspective of those trends that I have tried to see recent events; and to sketch future prospects. Only in this way is it possible, in my view, to find a thread leading through the labyrinth of contemporary history and the chaos of seemingly disconnected events.

I have been helped in this work by my wife. No acknowledgment can do justice to the contribution which her untiring patience, understanding, and critical mind have made. I am also greatly indebted to Miss Elizabeth Brommer for very many excellent stylistic suggestions.

My thanks are due to the Editors of the *Manchester Guardian*, *The Times*, and *The Reporter* (New York) who have kindly permitted me to reproduce some passages from my articles published in their pages.

Coulsdon, Surrey   I. D.
20 *April* 1953

CONTENTS

7

CONTENTS

PART ONE

THE BALANCE OF AN ERA

CHAPTER ONE

INTRODUCTION

WHEN Stalin died the whole world, wittingly or unwittingly, paid homage to the dead man and to the legend which hovered over his coffin. In the eyes of his followers he loomed even larger than Moses in the eyes of the Biblical Jews, for of Stalin his followers believed that he had actually led his people into the Promised Land. Most of his enemies, who saw in him Evil Incarnate, also in their way paid a tribute to Stalin by describing his departure as a momentous historical event, fraught with incalculable consequences. Of how many public figures could this be said with much conviction on the day of their death?

Involuntarily one is reminded of Shelley's lines 'On Hearing the News of the Death of Napoleon':

> How! is not *his* death-knell knolled?
> And livest *thou* still Mother Earth?
> Thou wert warming thy fingers old
> O'er the embers covered and cold
> Of that most fiery spirit, when it fled—
> What, Mother, do you laugh now he is dead?

Indeed, very few historical characters have had a comparable hold on the life and the imagination of their contemporaries. In an unsettled world, in an epoch of the most violent conflict and upheaval, in which so many dictators, rulers, regimes, governments, and parties one after another rose and in no time toppled to their ruin, Stalin alone ruled a vast country during nearly thirty years. He could well boast that his was the most stable government in the world, and he the best-established ruler of his time.

Yet, throughout most of his rule the oracles almost constantly predicted his imminent downfall. Not all of these were fools—there were among them sagacious and even great men. Stalin had in fact established his throne, as it were, on a volcano periodically shaken by deep convulsions—on the hot lava, and amid the fire and the smoke of the Russian revolution. At every rumbling of an explosion, onlookers expected that after the smoke had dispersed not a trace would be seen of Stalin. But each time Stalin was still there, in his old place, unscathed, and in a position more commanding and more awe inspiring than before; and at his feet lay the mangled bodies of his enemies and friends. He seemed to be the demigod in command of the volcano.

A whole Russian generation basked in his glory and trembled in his shadow. In the last fifteen years of his life, not only Russia but the whole world did the same. Popular imagination saw him holding the destiny of mankind in his hands.

How the son of a poor Georgian cobbler, a starving pupil of the Theological Seminary of Tiflis, a man outwardly so grey and inconspicuous, speaking in dry, scholastic formulæ, rose to this almost mythical grandeur will for ever fascinate the student of human affairs.

No wonder that after his death men should ask how large, for good or evil, is the gap Stalin has left, and how, if at all, it will be filled.

There are still those—and this writer is one of them—who do not subscribe to Carlyle's view of history and do not believe in mythical heroes and demigods. Without any desire to belittle the peculiar greatness of the man, it is still possible to think that much of the grandeur which surrounded him was one of those all too numerous optical illusions which circumstance and the human craving for illusion have combined to create and to fix into durable historical images. It may be held that at best

Stalin's grandeur reflected the magnitude of the issues and the vastness of the social processes underlying his career.

Those who take this view will prefer to approach the demigod soberly, to scrutinize his real features, to strip him of his Olympian garments, and to establish his genuine stature.

It is not intended here to follow Stalin through his life —this has been done by the writer elsewhere.[1] But it may be appropriate to draw now, if only tentatively, the balance of his life's work. It is surely in such a balance that an answer to the questions posed by Stalin's departure should be sought.

'There can be and there will be no change in the Soviet Union and in the Communist movement at large', the Stalinist now asserts, confident that Stalin's work will be carried on by his successors. 'Stalin is dead—long live Stalinism!' was the cry which resounded from Moscow over Stalin's open coffin.

Having for so long tried to persuade us that Stalin was the greatest genius in history, the Marx and the Lenin of his time, the Stalinist now suddenly, although discreetly, advances the classical Marxist argument that individuals do not matter in history, because they are only the agents and representatives of broader forces, of the social classes which are history's real moving forces. The peoples of the Soviet Union, we are told, have already found their new representative, mouthpiece, and leader, who will speak with Stalin's voice as Stalin had spoken with the voice of Lenin.

In this argument the Stalin cult achieves its own self-exposure: what it implies is that the Stalin cult was merely a propaganda stunt and a hoax. In truth, the Stalin

[1] I. Deutscher, *Stalin: A Political Biography* (Oxford University Press, 1949).

legend has been something more than this. But no matter how low a view one may take of it, the assurances that Stalin's death will entail no change in the Soviet Union are quite unconvincing, as we shall see later. Here it need only be observed in passing how foolishly the alleged adherents of dialectical materialism place the Soviet Union beyond and above all 'law of history'.

The whole world is supposed to be subject to dialectical change. Nothing in it is static. Everywhere rages the struggle of antagonistic elements which forms the essence of change. Everything is growth and decay. Only at the frontiers of the Stalinist realm is Dialectics refused an entry visa, apparently as a visitor suspect of un-Soviet activity. In Stalinist Russia there are and there can be no antagonistic elements, no contradictions, no processes of real change and transformation—only the harmonious evolution and perfection of society.

The Soviet realm is, of course, not immune from the laws of change to which the rest of this troubled world is subject. Moreover, despite some appearances to the contrary, these laws have been operating in Soviet Russia more intensively and on a vaster scale than elsewhere. By itself the death of even the most powerful ruler may not alter the fortunes of a country. But it may act as a catalyst in latent processes of change which have been in operation for some time. What is the real nature of these processes? And is Stalin's death likely to act on them as a catalyst? This is the chief subject of our inquiry.

The anti-Communist, who has been under the hypnosis of the Stalin legend in a negative way, also assures us that there will be no change in Russia. He points to the immutable façade of the Stalin regime and concludes that behind it everything has been frozen into immutability. He sees nothing but the simple picture of a will-less, helpless, cowed people of 200 millions (or even of 800 millions, if all Communist countries are considered), ruled by the tyrant's iron rod.

To those who adhere to this oversimplified view it

never occurs to ask how it could happen that nations which have in our century given so many striking proofs of their revolutionary frame of mind and temperament have become so meek and numb. How could it happen that the Russians who for a whole century threw bombs at their governors and ministers, chased their Tsars with revolvers, made three revolutions in the first two decades of this century, fought so many civil wars, and filled the world with the clangour of their arms—how these same Russians have become clay in the hands of a few men in the Kremlin? Or how could it happen that the Chinese, who also had shaken off dynasties, war-lords, and republican regimes and appeared incapable of settling down politically, have apparently come to accept Mao Tse-tung and have submitted to the rigorous discipline he has been imposing on them?

On a more sophisticated level the argument is advanced that our age has brought with it new techniques of government, which enable a totalitarian ruler to transform the most turbulent and rebellious nation into his plaything. Modern mass media of propaganda, all-pervading networks of spies, the power of the State as an employer, and the terror of concentration camps, so the argument runs, assure the stability of any totalitarian government. Such a government, it follows, can be overthrown only from outside, through defeat in war, as the regimes of Hitler and Mussolini have been overthrown. If so, then Stalin's death is an insignificant incident—the massive totalitarian machine will go on working in the background after it as before. A whole Soviet generation has already lived in Orwell's nightmare of *1984*; and it will go on doing so for an indefinite time.

It is difficult to deny the validity of this argument. Contemporary experience has, unfortunately, provided all too much evidence which appears to support it. But the argument also has its important flaws. Those who expound it tend to think of the primitive Russian society of the 1920's and early 1930's and of present-day China in terms applicable only to a highly industrialized and organized Western nation.

In the Russia of the 1920's and early 1930's—these were the formative years of the Stalinist regime and the years of its consolidation—the State was not yet the all-powerful employer. Nor is it in China today. The reference to the 'mass media' of totalitarian propaganda is even more irrelevant. In most Russian towns and villages of the early and middle Stalin era radio sets did not blare forth 'all-pervading' propaganda, simply because they were not available in sufficient numbers. Nor are they as yet available in China. In a primitive and largely illiterate nation, the influence of that other potent 'mass medium' of propaganda, the newspaper, is largely ineffective. Three-quarters of the Russian nation read no newspapers at the time when Stalin was setting up his totalitarian regime. Nor does the vast majority of the Chinese people read newspapers today.

All that may be said about the 'mass media' is that in a literate nation they are of the utmost importance to any aspirant to power; and that in an established totalitarian regime they are used to prevent or to slow down the formation of independent opinion. Even then their role is secondary—the success or failure of mass propaganda depends on a large variety of factors, not solely on the means of propaganda. The same is true of the instruments of political terror. These do not work in a vacuum. The effectiveness of their work depends largely on the nature of the material they work upon, and on the political morale of a country which can facilitate, obstruct or, in an extreme case, even bring to a standstill the machinery of terror.

Those who speak of the omnipotence of the totalitarian machine take a singularly unrealistic and superficial view of society, a curiously mechanical view which hardly befits writers who for the most part are so contemptuous of the materialist sociology of Marxism. They see only a single aspect of society—the mechanics of political power.

As a rule, they ignore the economic, social, cultural, psychological, and moral trends in a nation's life. Yet it is on these trends that the effectiveness of the mechanics of government largely depends. It is to them that we ought to turn our attention in order to find how they may affect the fortunes of Stalinism after Stalin. It will then be seen that it was the peculiar paradox of Stalinism that with one hand it fought ruthlessly and desperately to perpetuate its domination over the mind and the body of the Russian people and with the other it was, with equal ruthlessness and persistence, destroying the very pre-requisites of self-perpetuation. In other words, Stalin has done much, both negatively and positively, to ensure that Stalinism should not be able to survive him for very long.

In the weeks before and after Stalin's death, the news-papers were full of speculation about the secret rivalries in the Kremlin, the many-sided plots in which now Beria was supposed to be trying to oust Malenkov and Molotov, now Malenkov and Beria were supposed to oust Molotov, while in still other versions Bulganin and Beria were preparing a coup against all the others.

There were probably a few sparks behind this tremen-dous output of journalistic smoke. Not everything went smoothly within the walls of the Kremlin in the last weeks of Stalin's life, as the stories about the doctors' plot to assassinate some of the eminent personalities of the regime vaguely indicated.

Since Stalin's death it has often been suggested that the real government of the U.S.S.R. is exercised by a triumvirate or by another collegiate body similar to the triumvirate of Stalin-Zinoviev-Kamenev which assumed power after Lenin's departure.

Is it probable that history should repeat itself in such detail and that the pattern of events which followed Lenin's death should reproduce itself now?

The Russia of 1953 is very different from the Russia of 1924. The realities of power, the social structure, the political habits, the moral climate—all have changed almost beyond recognition, even though the phantoms of 1924 continue to hover over the Red Square. Yet there are some indications that before long Stalin's successor may try to chase away even those phantoms. He seems indeed to have begun the chase already.

Who is Malenkov? What does he represent? What does his ascendancy promise to Russia and the world?

In these pages an attempt will be made to sketch his career and character. This will not be easy. Until quite recently Malenkov's career ran its course behind the closed doors and the drawn curtains of Stalin's offices. But enough is known to provide some clues to Malenkov's personality and to the policies he is likely to pursue; and since his assumption of power he has given a few more clues, some of which are perhaps of greater significance than it appeared at first.

In what way Malenkov will act his part depends, however, less on himself than on the scene on which he has to act, on the forces in the background, and on the stage in the development of the plot at the moment of his entry. Once again then we have to take a broad view of the whole scene in order to approach the chief character and to see where he stands in relation to the heritage Stalin has left him.

It is tempting to speak of Stalinism at large and to forget that Stalinism was not a static, unchanging phenomenon. On the contrary, it passed through several distinct phases, each with its special features. It held under its sway several Soviet generations. Outwardly these generations may have appeared not to differ from one another. All have been steeped in the Stalin cult; and all seem to have behaved in the same way. Actually, the teachings, slogans, and myths of Stalinism have refracted themselves differently in the minds of each age group, for each has grown up in different social conditions.

What we are witnessing now is a crucial change of generations. The old Stalinist guard is gradually making its exit. What is the outlook of those who come to replace it? To what extent can they have developed new ideas and new aspirations? Where does Malenkov stand in relation to the changing generations?

In Stalinism, the Russian revolution was blended with age-old Russian tradition, as has been pointed out in detail elsewhere.[1] It seems therefore proper to look for possible precedents relevant to the present situation both in the history of modern revolutions and in Russia's own past.

We know of only one significant instance in which a revolutionary-republican dictator tried to bequeath immense power and authority to a chosen heir. In seventeenth-century England, Oliver Cromwell attempted to pass on the heritage of the Puritan revolution and of the Protectorate to his son Richard. However, very soon after Cromwell's death, his soldiers overthrew the son, restored the Stuarts to their throne, and acclaimed the returning Charles II at least as jubilantly as they had once applauded the execution of Charles I. Is it possible that Malenkov should be Stalin's Richard?

In Russian history there are the memories of what happened after the death of Ivan the Terrible and Peter the Great, the two Tsars with whom Stalin has often been compared. Under both these Tsars, Russia's power had grown immensely and her outlook had undergone profound changes, many of which survived their initiators and profoundly influenced posterity. Yet after each of these Tsars, Russia's power receded and shrank. Is there any reason to suppose that something similar may occur again?

One may also recall another Russian precedent. Under Nicholas I, the Iron Tsar, Russia seemed as if frozen in

[1] See my *Stalin*.

the tyranny of her ruler and in—immobility. Thus Western observers saw her. Yet underneath the surface, influences were at work which made for change. Only a few years after the close of the reign of Nicholas I, his successor Alexander II emancipated the Russian and the Polish peasant-serfs and introduced a number of quasi-liberal reforms.

No doubt to some extent every precedent may be irrelevant to the present situation. The parallels drawn from Russian history relate to regimes which were not revolutionary in origin and character, despite the sweeping reforms carried out by the rulers. The analogies drawn from other revolutions may be partly invalidated by the different nature of the Russian revolution, and by the fact that no previous revolution, not even the French in its Napoleonic phase, had spread over as vast a portion of the globe as that which is now under the sway of Stalinism. Whither then is the Russian revolution going as its fourth decade draws to a close?

These are the questions to be probed. But enough has perhaps already been said to foreshadow the general answer:

It is implausible to expect that Stalin's immediate successor will be merely Stalin's continuator. No doubt, he will keep up the pretence of being just that, as Stalin kept up the pretence that he was merely Lenin's continuator. In truth, Stalinism was a continuation of Leninism only in some respects. In others it represented a radical departure from it. There is reason to think that whatever comes in Russia now will only be in part a continuation of Stalinism, while in some vital respects it will mark a break with the Stalin era.

CHAPTER TWO

FROM LENINISM TO STALINISM

THE forecast of a break with the Stalinist era at once brings the sceptic to his feet: 'Surely', he says, 'you are making a sweeping statement? On what can you possibly base it? Only on the accident of Stalin's death in March 1953?'

No, not only on this accident. Of Stalin, one can only say what George Plekhanov, the great Russian thinker, once wrote about other historic figures: 'Owing to the specific qualities of their minds and characters, influential individuals can change the *individual features of events and some of their particular consequences*, but they cannot change their general *trend*, which is determined by other forces.'

It is the 'general trend' of contemporary Soviet life which has been preparing the break with the Stalin era; and Stalin's death and its consequences can only influence some 'individual features' of the process.

The prediction is less sweeping than may at first appear when it is added that the break with the Stalin era is likely to be similar to that by which Stalinism disengaged itself from the Leninist era of Bolshevism.

Stalinism developed out of Leninism, preserving some of the features of Leninism and discarding others. It continued in the Leninist tradition; but it also stood in a bitter and unavowed opposition to it. Whatever trend emerges in Russia in the near future is likely to adopt the same dual and ambivalent attitude towards Stalinism, preserving some of its features, modifying others, and discarding still others.

A crisis of Stalinism has been latent for some time past. All that Stalin's death can do is to bring the crisis into the open, partly or wholly, and to underline the need for a solution. Stalin, like Lenin before him, died at a crossroad of Bolshevik history.

To understand the nature of this crossroads it may be useful to cast a glance back upon the road which Russia has traversed in the last three decades, and upon the starting-point of that road—the transition from Leninism to Stalinism. The heritage of the Stalin era and Russia's attitude towards it may then be seen in perspective.

At the time of Lenin's illness and death (1922–4), Bolshevism was in the throes of a profound crisis, which was aggravated but by no means brought about by Lenin's disappearance. The Russian revolution was no longer able to travel along the road on which Lenin had led it. If Lenin had lived longer he would hardly have been in a position to go on leading it along the same road. He would have been compelled to change direction, one way or another; and his departure speeded up the change.

The crisis in Bolshevik affairs which coincided with Lenin's death affected the domestic and foreign policies of Bolshevism, and indeed its whole moral climate.

Lenin had been brought up in the old Marxist school of thought, which had come into being in Western Europe, when Western Europe was leading the world in industrial development. The Marxian ideas of the proletarian revolution, the proletarian dictatorship, and the character of a socialist economy were working hypotheses designed to fit a highly industrialized, civilized, and organized capitalist society, with a very strongly developed industrial working class. In the view of nearly all the early Russian Marxists these ideas had no immediate practical relevance to Russia. Until very late in his career, up to the First World War, Lenin refused even to countenance any thought about a socialist revolution in Russia in any foreseeable future.

Only shortly before 1917 did he change his mind and

adopt the view that the Russian revolution would have
to overthrow not merely Tsardom and what had remained of the feudal order, as he had thought hitherto,
but the underdeveloped Russian capitalism as well.

For a whole century Russia had been fraught with
revolution; but the revolutionary movement had been led
by an intelligentsia which had had almost no following
among the broader classes of the nation. Since the turn
of the century, however, the young, small, but politically
very active Russian working class had become 'the chief
driving force' of the revolution. The workers could not
be expected to content themselves with the overthrow of
the Tsar and of the landed gentry, to whom they were
opposed only indirectly. They saw the capitalist indus-
trialists as their immediate enemies; and in a revolutionary situation they were bound to aim at the expropriation
and the overthrow of the latter. This, however, would
mark the beginning of a socialist revolution, leading to
the establishment of a nationalized and planned economy.
Such was Lenin's attitude at the outbreak of the revolution of 1917.

But it was still Lenin's (and his party's) conviction
that Russia's industrial resources and the general level of
her civilization were highly inadequate for the establishment of socialism. Thus Lenin expounded the idea of a
socialist revolution in Russia and he himself led the
revolution while recognizing that if victorious the movement could not achieve its ultimate purpose in Russia.

This was a fundamental contradiction in his attitude.
He sought to resolve it by treating the Russian revolution as the first act of a much wider international upheaval, the main arena of which he saw, in accordance
with Marxist tradition, in the industrial countries of
Western Europe.

The Russian revolution was therefore, in Lenin's
view, no self-sufficient, national-Russian phenomenon;
and the chances of the future socialist order were not
dependent on the inadequate resources of Russia alone.

Western industry, technology, and civilization were to supply the basis and the elements of socialism; and Russia, raised up industrially and culturally with the help of Western revolutionary States, was to participate in the experience and the benefits of an international socialist order.

This was no mere theoretical construction. The whole emotional content of Bolshevism in 1917 and after centred on the expectation of a more or less imminent revolution in the West. Lenin and his associates were not the original authors of the prognostication about the impending downfall of Western capitalism. Nor did they for a moment imagine that it was they who could bring it about. A whole generation of European, especially German, social democrats had grown up in the belief that capitalism had outlived its day in the West. Karl Kautsky, the intellectual inspirer of that generation, the man whose modest disciple Lenin regarded himself up to 1914, had argued along these lines ever since the beginning of the century.

But most Western European Marxists treated their own prognostications as ritualistic performances, as something like socialist variations on the Christian theme of the Last Judgment. They refused to be guided in their practical policies by their own preachings. In the pre-1914 Socialist International, the future leaders of the Russian revolution formed almost the only party which believed with passion and zeal in the near advent of international revolution. On this belief the Bolsheviks staked their actions and their—heads.

Lenin's death coincided with a crisis in this belief. From 1918 till 1923, in the aftermath of the First World War, the revolutionary ferment which had engulfed Europe still kept the flame of that belief burning. But the old order, slightly reformed, managed to survive in Europe; and by 1924 the revolutionary ferment had subsided. The Russian revolution was to remain isolated for an indefinite time. The Bolshevik assumptions appeared to have been refuted by the events. Bolshevik Russia had to adapt herself to her isolation.

The dilemma to which this gave rise was in the centre of the struggle between Stalin and Trotsky. To use terms now current, Bolshevism had to decide whether it should go on staking its future on the 'liberation', that is on the self-emancipation, of foreign working classes or whether it ought to aim at 'containing' capitalism at the frontiers of the Soviet Union. The policy of 'liberation' appeared to have exhausted its possibilities: the working classes in foreign countries were neither ready nor willing to overthrow capitalism. Soviet policy moved slowly but irresistibly towards 'containment', which involved a radical revision of Leninist assumptions and attitudes.

It remains a moot point whether Lenin himself would have been able to carry out such a revision, which would have gone against all his mental habits and cardinal beliefs. Rarely, if ever, has an initiator of a great revolutionary movement been able to throw overboard his cherished ideas and principles when these clashed with immediate reality or had been outpaced by events. The Russian revolution was withdrawing into its national shell; and Lenin, the internationalist *par excellence*, might not have been able to withdraw with it. At any rate, the great majority of his friends and disciples, who by his side had led the October Revolution and had built the Soviet State, found themselves at loggerheads with the new trend in Bolshevism.

Lenin died at a moment when history had overtaken him. His illness and death relieved him of the bitter necessity to grapple with a dilemma which he might have found insoluble.

The crisis which confronted Leninism in its domestic policy was no less deep and grave. There, too, Lenin's party was marking time at a crossroad, while Lenin was on his deathbed.

Bolshevism had proclaimed the 'proletarian dictatorship' in Russia; but it had also conceived that dictatorship as a 'proletarian democracy'. To put it in simpler terms, Lenin had frankly and without inhibition denied any political freedom to the former possessing and ruling classes and to their parties. His government, like any revolutionary government before it, claimed the right to suppress those who strove, arms in hand, to restore the pre-revolutionary order. This was the meaning of proletarian dictatorship.

But Leninism also committed itself in 1917 and afterwards to respect, to guard, to promote, and to extend in every possible way the political freedom of the working classes, who should have been the real masters in the new State. This was the meaning of 'proletarian democracy', which should have supplemented, or rather formed the basis of, the dictatorship.

However, during the civil war, and even more so after it, the political freedoms of the working classes too were gradually curtailed and largely destroyed. This is not the place to explain and analyse this development.[1] Suffice it to say here that towards the end of the Leninist era the dictatorship spoke on behalf of the proletariat but that only a residuum of proletarian democracy had survived. The Bolsheviks had outlawed all rival parties, including the Mensheviks and Anarchists, who had had their main following among the workers, and the Social Revolutionaries, who had drawn their support from the peasantry.

True enough, those parties had, because of their antirevolutionary attitude, forfeited most or nearly all of their support among the working classes. But in a proletarian democracy, as the Bolsheviks originally conceived it, those parties should have been allowed to go on competing with the Bolsheviks for influence over the masses. This they were not allowed to do.

Lenin had never made a principle of the single party

[1] For this description and analysis I must refer the reader to my forthcoming book *The Prophet Armed*, which is a biographical study of Trotsky.

system; yet towards the end of his life the Soviet regime had become just such a system. The abolition of 'proletarian democracy' could not leave unaffected the Bolshevik Party itself, which now proceeded to curtail the freedom of expression in its own ranks, for its own members.

The trend was leading from a proletarian democracy towards an autocracy speaking on behalf of the proletariat.

Yet the idea of proletarian democracy had been deeply rooted in the mind of the party. Lenin had proposed each of the successive restrictions of proletarian democracy as an emergency measure, to be cancelled after the emergency was over. During the civil war he outlawed the Mensheviks, the Social Revolutionaries, and other minor groups; then he allowed them to come into the open again and to renew activity; and then he drove them finally underground. Internal freedom in the Bolshevik Party survived the civil war; but it began to shrink rapidly soon afterwards. Emergency followed emergency, and the restrictive measures at first designed to be temporary came to stay.

The direction in which the regime was evolving disturbed profoundly important sections of the Bolshevik Party. Towards the end of the Leninist era the party was internally divided over this issue. Some of its leaders and members clamoured for a return to proletarian democracy, although only very few went so far as to demand the restoration of freedom to the defeated enemies of the revolution. Others strove to arrest halfway the drift towards a quasi-socialist autocracy. Still others, from conviction or self-interest or both, promoted the prevalent trend, saying or implying that the restoration of political freedoms would wreck the revolution, and that its safety lay in a further concentration of power at the top, in the Central Committee, in the Politbureau, and eventually in the hands of a single leader. Bolshevism was torn between its democratic past and its undemocratic future.

42766

Lenin's position in this controversy was extremely difficult. He had been responsible for the measures which restricted the freedom of expression even of those who had supported the revolution; and he had also been the standard-bearer of proletarian democracy. He tried to strike a balance between dictatorship and democracy. He himself did not rule his party with an iron rod. He dominated it by the sheer weight of his intellectual and moral authority. At all the party congresses over which he presided, he was openly assailed by many and sometimes very influential opponents. On occasions he was outvoted and then he either submitted to the majority or sought to reverse its decision by constitutional means.

In his last years Lenin struggled to arrest halfway the trend from proletarian democracy towards an autocracy. But the trend was to prove stronger—it could no longer be arrested, let alone reversed. In nothing was this demonstrated more strikingly than in the story of Lenin's will. In it Lenin advised his followers to remove Stalin from the post of the party's General Secretary on the ground that Stalin had gathered too much power in his hands and was making too brutal a use of it. Lenin's advice had no effect. His successors ignored it and brushed it aside at the same time as they were initiating a quasi-religious cult of the dead Lenin.

If Lenin had lived longer he could not have grappled with the dilemma indefinitely, for otherwise the trend would have overpowered or by-passed him. He would have had to make up his mind either in favour of a gradual restoration of proletarian democracy or in favour of an autocratic form of government, and then he himself would have had to become the autocrat. In other words, he would have had to do either what Trotsky did or what Stalin did. In Lenin's personality both these characters were in a sense blended; and it is at least doubtful whether he could have become either a Trotsky or a Stalin, without disintegrating his whole personality.

Thus once again we see how the death of a great

leader coincided with a crucial ferment, which was to
drive his party from its accustomed road, to cause an
upheaval in its outlook and its moral climate, and to re-
group its leading personnel. The accident of Lenin's
death in 1924 can be seen as 'something relative', to
paraphrase Plekhanov. It occurred 'at the point of
intersection of inevitable events'.

So did Stalin's rise to power. More than any other
Bolshevik leader, Stalin was determined to solve the
crisis of Bolshevism in a definite manner, without hark-
ing back unduly to the party's traditions, without giving
himself to theoretical scruple or—human weakness. The
fact that he made a cult of Leninism does not contradict
this assertion. It was only by doing so that he could
render Leninism harmless and irrelevant to practical
policy. The Leninist tradition had dominated the party
so strongly that the only way of effectively breaking away
from that tradition was to present even that break as an
act of devotion.

In one fundamental respect Stalin did, of course, continue Lenin's work. He strove to preserve the State
founded by Lenin and to increase its might. He also
preserved and then expanded the nationalized and State-
managed industry, in which the Bolsheviks saw the basic
framework of their new society. These important threads
of continuity between Leninism and Stalinism were
never cut.

But when Stalin took over its direction the State was in
such a condition that it could be preserved only by being
politically refashioned almost into its opposite. In theory
it might still have become either a proletarian democracy
or an autocracy. In fact only one road was open to it: the
one leading towards autocracy.

The Bolshevik regime could not revert to its democratic origin, because it could not hope for enough
democratic support to guarantee its survival. After the
civil wars, with their legacy of destruction, poverty, and
famine, there was too much acute discontent in the classes

which had helped the Bolsheviks to win these wars for the Bolsheviks to rely on their backing. In later years, when economic reconstruction was under way and the ruling group might have met with more popular support, its members were already fixed in undemocratic habits of government and had a stake in persisting in those habits. It is as a rule easier for any government or party to move away from a democratic principle a thousand miles than to go back to it a single yard.

Stalin was not inclined to go back a single inch. He identified himself wholeheartedly and unreservedly with the development towards autocracy. He became its chief promoter and its chief beneficiary. Unswervingly he re-moulded the Leninist State into a new, authoritarian-bureaucratic shape.

He had even less hesitation in breaking away from the revolutionary internationalist aspect of Leninism.

During the Leninist period he had, like every other Bolshevik, expounded the view that the Russian revolution could not be self-sufficient, and that its future depended on the progress of world revolution. He emphatically repeated this even shortly after Lenin's death, saying that socialism could not be built up in a single isolated country, especially in one as 'backward' as Russia.

Even while he was reiterating this Leninist axiom, world revolution was to him merely an abstract idea. The immediate reality in which he was wholly immersed, and to which he genuinely responded, was the Russian revolution. The other party leaders, who as émigrés had lived many years in the West and had been impressed by its seemingly powerful Marxist movement, could argue with great sincerity that international communism had first claim on Soviet Russia, or even that the interests of Soviet Russia had to be subordinated to those of world revolution. To Stalin this reasoning was little better than a mental aberration of émigrés, on whom the West had cast a magic spell, depriving them of any sense of reality.

Instinctively he adopted an attitude towards which the Russian revolution was in any case drifting, an attitude of national self-centredness and self-sufficiency. To many rank and file Bolsheviks world revolution had become a lamentable myth by 1924, while the building of socialism in Russia was the exacting and exhilarating experience of their generation. Despite all his verbal tributes to Leninist internationalism, Stalin became the chief mouthpiece of this sentiment. He elevated the sacred egoism of the Russian revolution to a supreme principle —this was the real meaning of his idea of 'socialism in one country'. He was determined to make the sacred egoism of the 'only proletarian State in the world' the guiding idea of international communism as well. Whenever the interests of foreign communism clashed or appeared to clash with those of the Soviet Union, he sacrificed foreign communism.

By the middle of the 1920's Bolshevism had virtually solved its dilemma of 'liberation' versus 'containment' in favour of containment. World capitalism was not to be allowed to overlap the frontiers of the Soviet Union. But the Soviet Union was not to forgo even the slightest chance of an understanding with any bourgeois government, even if such an understanding could be bought only at the price of 'betraying' foreign communism. Fascist regimes, bourgeois democracies, and Oriental reactionary dictatorships—all were equally good, or equally bad, as partners in trade and diplomatic bargaining.

The Communist International still proudly claiming to be the vanguard of world revolution became the rearguard of Stalin's diplomacy. It was used as an instrument of Soviet pressure upon capitalist governments rather than as a militant movement fighting for their overthrow.

'Socialism in one country' was in effect the formula in which Bolshevism, under Stalin's leadership, intimated its readiness for *self-containment* to a world which was anyhow bent on containing it. Thus the statesmen of the Western world understood the formula; and most of them applauded Stalin's victory over Trotsky, in whom they saw the hateful incarnation of all the world-revolutionary aspirations of early Bolshevism. (Little did those statesmen expect that one day they would feel threatened by a revolution carried on the point of the bayonets of Stalin's armies!)

As long as Bolshevism hoped and believed that its ultimate salvation would come from abroad, it remained in a sense elevated above its Russian environment. It did not feel dependent on that environment only. It could afford to express its disdain for native 'backwardness', for Russia's semi-Asiatic outlook, and for her Tsarist past; and nobody vented that disdain more often and with less inhibition than Lenin did. During the early years of the Soviet regime, the Bolshevik leaders had the feeling that they were Marxists *in partibus infidelium*, West European revolutionaries acting against a non-congenial Oriental background, which temporarily restricted their freedom of movement and tried to impose its tyranny upon them. Only revolution in the West could relieve them from that tyranny; and that it was about to do so was beyond doubt.

No sooner had Bolshevism mentally withdrawn into its national shell than this attitude became untenable. The party of the revolution had to stoop to its semi-Asiatic environment. It had to cut itself loose from the specifically Western tradition of Marxism. It had to lay itself open to the slow, persistent infiltration of native backwardness and barbarism, even while it struggled to defeat that backwardness and barbarism.

The adjustment began in the early part of the Stalinist era, and it did so in every field of activity: in the method of government, in the approach to problems of culture and education, in the relations with the outside world, in the style of diplomatic dealings, and so on. The process of infiltration was gaining momentum throughout the Stalinist era; and it reached a grotesque climax just at its end.

This does not mean that Bolshevism surrendered to its native environment. On the contrary, during the greater part of the Stalin era Bolshevism was as if at war with it—industrializing, collectivizing, and modernizing it. In a sense, Bolshevism has 'Westernized' the essential framework of Russian society. But it could do so only by itself becoming 'Orientalized'. This mutual interpenetration of modern technology and Marxist socialism with Russian barbarism formed the content of the Stalin era.

Shortly before his death Lenin had a premonition of the shape of things to come. He recalled the familiar historical phenomenon when a nation which has conquered another nation culturally superior to it succumbs to the political and cultural standards of the conquered. Something similar, so Lenin argued, may happen in class struggle: an oppressed and uneducated class may overthrow a ruling class culturally superior to it; and then the defeated class may impose its own standards upon the victorious revolutionary forces. In a flash of extraordinary foresight, Lenin had the vision of his disciples, the former professional revolutionaries, adopting the methods of government and the standards of behaviour of the Tsars, the feudal *boyars*, and the old bureaucracy. Lenin warned his followers against this danger; but up to a point he himself furthered it. He argued, for instance, that in order to prepare Russia for socialism industrially, technologically, and educationally, Bolshevism must drive barbarism out of Russia by barbarous methods, as Peter the Great had done in his time.

This *obiter dictum*, one of Lenin's many and sometimes contradictory sayings, became Stalin's guiding principle. He had none of the qualms about barbarous methods which beset Lenin and other Bolshevik leaders; and he had no hesitation in proclaiming that the driving out of barbarism in a barbarous manner was no mere preliminary to socialism—it was socialism itself.

To sum up: the transition from Leninism to Stalinism consisted in the abandonment of a revolutionary internationalist tradition in favour of the sacred egoism of Soviet Russia; and in the suppression of Bolshevism's pristine attachment to proletarian democracy in favour of an autocratic system of government. The isolation of the Russian revolution resulted in its mental self-isolation and in its spiritual and political adaptation to primordial Russian tradition. Stalinism represented the amalgamation of Western European Marxism with Russian barbarism.

A brief historical digression may perhaps be permitted here.

We have seen that Marxist communism had had its cradle in the industrial West. A Western philosophy (Hegel), a Western political economy (Ricardo), and the ideas of Western Utopian socialism (Saint-Simon, Fourier, Owen) had nursed it. Marxism claimed to make articulate theoretically and to express politically the revolutionary aspirations of Western industrial workers. During many decades it then strove to convert and conquer the West through the exertions of the Western working classes. By the turn of the century great labour movements had sprung up all over Western Europe, which marched under Marxist banners and solemnly vowed to use their first opportunity to carry out proletarian revolutions.

Yet this apparent success of Marxism was spurious. More than a hundred years after the message of the *Communist Manifesto* had first resounded throughout the world not a single proletarian revolution has triumphed in the West. Not even a single full-scale attempt at such a revolution, an attempt genuinely backed by a majority of the working class, has taken place in the West, apart from the Commune of Paris, defeated in 1871.

Instead Marxism has spread to the East; and by the efforts of the intelligentsia and a young and small working class it has conquered primitive peasant nations, from whom it had expected little or no response, and whom it had not considered capable of initiating a socialist order. At the middle of this century Marxism has become in a sense displaced from the West and naturalized in Russia and China. Where it has survived as a mass movement in the West, in France and Italy, it has done so in its 'Orientalized' form; and it exists there as a broad reflex of the Russian metamorphosis of Marxism.

In the East Marxism has absorbed the traditions of Tsardom and of Greek Orthodoxy. It has indeed become so thoroughly transformed that the West has almost forgotten that Marxism is its own authentic product and has come to treat it almost as if it were an exotic Oriental religion.[1] In its prevalent Stalinist version Marxism has very nearly ceased to understand the West, and has itself become incomprehensible to the West. So profound has become the displacement and transformation of the greatest revolutionary and international movement of our age.

A striking parallel to this is found in the fortunes of early Christianity, which came into being as a Judaic 'heresy', as one of the extreme sects in the Synagogue, wholly in character with old Biblical tradition, and bent on converting to its beliefs primarily the Jews. Yet it was not given to Christianity to convert the people from whose midst its Man-God and its Apostles had come. Instead, Christianity moved into a disintegrating pagan world, whose mind was no longer dominated by the old gods, where Jupiter's thunder no longer made men

---

[1] Only quite recently Professor Arnold Toynbee brought upon himself some criticism because he described Communism as a Western—or even a Christian—'heresy'.

tremble, and Neptune was no longer able to shake the seas.

It was in the temples of the old Græco-Roman deities that Christianity made its conquests; and it began to breathe the air of their temples, to absorb and assimilate pagan myths, symbols, and beliefs. It came to dominate its new environment while it was adapting itself to it. It ceased to be a Jewish heresy; it ceased to live on the Nazarene memories of the Old Testament and on Jewish oral tradition. It ceased to understand the Jews and it became incomprehensible to the Jews. From the Judaic creed of the oppressed it became the religion of the Roman Cæsars. But converting the Cæsars, it also became converted to Cæsarism, until the Holy See became an Imperial court, and until the hierarchical habits of the Roman Empire became its ecclesiastic canons.

In Christianity this evolution lasted centuries; in Bolshevism—only decades. If Lenin was the St. Paul of Marxism, who set out to transplant the movement from its original environment into new lands, Stalin was already its Constantine the Great. He was, to be sure, not the first Emperor to embrace Marxism, but the first Marxist revolutionary to become the autocratic ruler of a vast empire.

CHAPTER THREE

MARXISM AND PRIMITIVE MAGIC

PLEKHANOV, whom we have already quoted, wrote that if historical circumstances create the need for a certain political function to be performed they also supply the 'organ' capable of performing it. If the need for the 'function' is deeply rooted in the conditions of an epoch, the epoch is sure to bring forth not just one but at least several individuals with the minds, the characters, and the wills needed to perform the function. As a rule, circumstances allow only one or, at the most, a few of a whole group of potential leaders to move to the front of the stage; and so the historical record contains the evidence only of their capabilities and deeds. The fact that one individual has already filled the place of the actual leader debars other potential leaders from revealing themselves—they are condemned to remain in obscurity.

Plekhanov applied this theory not only to politics. He argued, for instance, that if Leonardo da Vinci had not lived to produce his masterpieces, this would not have altered the broad trend of the artistic ideas of the Renaissance, because this trend had sprung from the social conditions and from the intellectual and moral climate of the age. Only the 'individual features' of the trend would have been different. The same is true of the great scientific discoveries which bear the name of a single man. Such discoveries are the outcome of the stage of development which a certain branch of science has reached at a particular time, and it is more or less a matter of chance which individual actually makes them. Indeed, it often happens that several leading scientists make a discovery almost simultaneously and independently of one another.

To return to political history: if, for instance, a certain General Bonaparte had been killed in a battle before he had time to become First Consul and Emperor of revolutionary France, another general would have filled his place with essentially the same effect. There were in France at that time several military leaders capable of this. Bonaparte's rise prevented those potential Napoleons from becoming actual ones. The 'organ' capable of performing the historical 'function' had been supplied; and there was no room for duplication. That 'function' consisted in giving an authoritarian and yet revolutionary government—the rule of a 'good sword'—to a nation which had tried out and abandoned the republican-plebeian democracy of the Jacobins but still refused to countenance the restoration of the pre-revolutionary order.

Plekhanov's argument has given rise to considerable controversy, into which it is not proposed to enter here. Suffice it to say that even among Marxists, who broadly accepted Plekhanov's view, there have been many 'deviations' from it.

Trotsky, for instance, in his *History of the Russian Revolution*, attempted to strike a balance between the general Marxist philosophy of history—which sees the collective forces of social classes and groups as the decisive agents in any historical process—and his own view that Lenin's individual role in the Russian revolution was unique, that is to say that no other Bolshevik leader would have been qualified to perform it. However, Trotsky 'deviated' even further from the classical Plekhanovist view. In a private letter to an old Bolshevik friend which he wrote from his exile in Alma Ata, he stated bluntly and without inhibition: 'You know that without Lenin the October Revolution would not have won.'[1] Thus, while in his published writings he tried to adjust his own view of Lenin's role with Plekhanov's theory, privately he appears to have taken an attitude diametrically opposed to it.

The story of Stalin's career seems calculated to resolve the controversy in favour of Plekhanov.

Hardly any of Stalin's contemporaries, comrades and rivals alike, regarded him at first as in any way suited to the role he was to play. He appeared to them to have none of the gifts which make a great leader, Bolshevik or otherwise. His ascendancy came as a complete surprise. Trotsky wrote of Stalin that he detached himself like a shadow from a Kremlin wall to succeed Lenin. This impression was shared by Zinoviev, Kamenev, Rykov, Tomsky, Bukharin, and also by nearly all the leaders of the non-Russian Communist Parties.[2] Lenin alone was more discerning in his appraisal of the man, for although eventually he advised his followers to depose Stalin from the post of the party's General Secretary, he nevertheless described both Stalin and Trotsky as the 'two ablest men' in the Central Committee.

Why was it that nearly everyone who had known Stalin before and during his rise was so utterly wrong about his chances?

The typical Bolshevik leader of the Leninist era was, as a rule, a Marxist theorist, a political strategist, a fluent writer, and an effective orator, in addition to being some sort of organizer. Stalin did not count at all as a theorist.[3]

[1] The writer found this letter in the Trotsky Archives at Harvard.

[2] This was, of course, even more true of the anti-communists. Thus the Menshevik *Sotsialisticheskii Vestnik* wrote after Stalin's death: 'We, who have known personally and often quite closely the leaders of the Bolshevik Party since 1903, and who have met also Stalin as early as 1906 and later have wondered more than once how it happened that all of us . . . could so underrate him. Nobody thought of him as an eminent political worker. . . .' (*Sotsialisticheskii Vestnik*, February-March 1953.)

[3] It is possible to prove from the internal evidence of Stalin's writings that he became acquainted with Marx's *Das Kapital* only towards the end of his life.

He was to the end a political tactician rather than a strategist: he showed his mastery in short-term manœuvre rather than in long-term conception, although his genius for tactics did more than compensate his weakness as a strategist. He was cumbersome and ineffective as a writer and speaker. Only as an exceptionally gifted organizer had he made his mark in Lenin's lifetime. His contemporaries and rivals had reason therefore to think that he was unfit to be Lenin's successor.

Their mistake lay in the assumption that Bolshevik Russia after Lenin needed the type of leadership which Lenin had provided and which Lenin's closest associates might have provided collectively or individually. They misjudged the changing circumstances and the new need of the time; and so they failed to see that the man who might not have been qualified to act as the leader in one phase of the revolution might be eminently suited for that role in the subsequent phase.

We know that among those changing circumstances Bolshevik Russia's political isolation in the world and mental self-isolation from it were the most important. The isolation was not of Stalin's making—it was a consequence of events preceding his ascendancy. He merely took the situation as it was. He was reconciled to it and inwardly free to act within its framework; and therefore he thrived on it. Most of his rivals were unreconciled to Russia's isolation, incapable of overcoming their internationalist habits of thought, and not disposed to frame policies consistently within the context of isolation. They were at odds with the root fact of the new time; and they were undone by it.

The same is true of Stalin's as against his rivals' attitude in the dilemma of proletarian democracy *versus* autocracy, the other crucial issue in the transition from Leninism to Stalinism. It was not Stalin who had destroyed the proletarian democracy of the early phase of the revolution. It had withered even before 1923–4; at most, Stalin delivered the *coup de grace*.

His rivals, however, could not shed their democratic habits. They were not inwardly reconciled to the fact that, struggling for the preservation of its revolution, Bolshevism had deprived the working classes of freedom of political expression. They were entangled in their own regrets, scruples, and second thoughts. They looked back longingly to the democratic origins of the revolution. Stalin did nothing of the sort. They were therefore not fitted to act effectively within the new, undemocratic framework of the Bolshevik State. He was. They were crushed by that framework, while he proceeded to build around it his autocratic system of government.[1]

The trend of the time found in Stalin its 'organ'. If it hadn't been Stalin it would have been another.

A similar view when expressed about other historical figures may seem implausible; but it is exceptionally convincing in the case of Stalin.

When it is said that the general trend of the Renaissance would not have been different without Leonardo da Vinci and that at the most some of its 'individual features' would have been different, one immediately thinks of the 'Last Supper' and 'Mona Lisa,' and one wonders: Would the trend really not have been different? Was the contribution of Leonardo (or of Michelangelo) merely one of its 'individual features'?

When one is told that another French general of the period of the Directory could have filled the place of Napoleon, one cannot help thinking about Napoleon's élan, intellectual brilliance, and romantic appeal; and one

---

[1] It is interesting to note here the view of Mr. R. Abramovich, the Menshevik veteran who could well celebrate now the fifty years' jubilee of his uninterrupted and increasingly vehement struggle against Bolshevism. In the article from the *Sotsialisticheskii Vestnik*, quoted above, Mr. Abramovich (we assume he is its author) writes: 'Thinking about the past it seems to us that the basic reason of our common, evidently incorrect appraisal of Stalin's personality was that we thought in terms of a democratic system, and strangely enough not only we, the Mensheviks, the opponents of the dictatorship, but *also its adherents* did so.' (My italics—I.D.)

wonders just how much Napoleon's individual characteristics counted in the general course of events.

But when one contemplates Stalin, that grey, inconspicuous, almost faceless character, one is more than inclined to see in him but the vehicle of anonymous forces at work in the background. He appears as the embodiment of Anonymity itself, Anonymity which rose to the pinnacle of power and fame and even there remained true to itself—utterly impersonal and therefore utterly elusive.

When the struggle between Stalin and Trotsky is viewed only in terms of individual gifts and talents, Stalin's victory over his rival remains inexplicable. Stalin had not a single gift that Trotsky did not possess in the same or in a much higher degree; in addition Trotsky had conspicuous talents which Stalin altogether lacked. It was no exaggeration when Lenin, a great judge of men, described Trotsky as 'the ablest' of all the Bolshevik leaders.

It is often said that Trotsky did not have Stalin's flair for organization. Nobody who has studied the history of the Red Army can seriously entertain that view. In so far as any single individual may be credited with this achievement, Trotsky was the true organizer of the army. He created it 'from nothing' after the old army had collapsed, dissolved, and left a military vacuum. To fill the vacuum with a new army demanded a genius for organization and administration superior to that required for making even the most effective use of an already existing and well-established army. After the Red Army had come into being there was hardly a military authority, Russian or non-Russian, Bolshevik or anti-Bolshevik, who did not describe Trotsky's feat as 'truly Napoleonic'.[1]

---

[1] This is, for instance, how General Ludendorff and General Hoffmann, the outstanding commanders of the German Army in the First World War and Trotsky's enemies during the Brest Litovsk period, described his military achievement.

It is also said that Stalin was superior to Trotsky as a political tactician. Again, it is enough to study from original sources the tactical manœuvres which Trotsky carried out on the eve of the October Revolution, and during the revolution itself, to realize that this too is incorrect. As the operational leader of the Bolshevik insurrection, Trotsky almost alone—Lenin was then in hiding—lulled and hypnotized all the enemies of the Bolshevik Party into a state of utter inactivity, and even into complicity with the Bolsheviks. He won the insurrection almost without firing a shot: its most hostile eye-witnesses did not put the number of casualties on both sides at more than ten.

Stalin, on the other hand, made no mark as a tactician in 1917; and, as the records of the Bolshevik Central Committee show, he did not put forward a single tactical idea throughout that year.

Yet it is true that in his struggle against Stalin Trotsky was always tactically inferior.

The question must therefore be asked: What made Trotsky, the genius in tactics of 1917, into the inferior tactician of 1924–7? And what made Stalin, the indifferent tactician of 1917, into the master of the later years?

The answer may be found in the different general conditions of the two periods, in consequence of which Trotsky, not Stalin, was in his element in 1917, while Stalin, not Trotsky, was in his some years later.

Stalin was fitted for his role not merely and not even primarily by his great talents for organization and tactics. His background, his experience, and his cast of mind had prepared him to lead Bolshevism in the break with its democratic origins and through the decades of its isolation and self-isolation. For the 'function' of such a leadership he was the most perfect 'organ'.

He had spent all his years inside Russia, mostly in his native Caucasus on the borders of Europe and Asia, where he had been insulated from the direct influences of Western European Marxism. This was his weakness during the Leninist period, when Bolshevism was staking its future on revolution in the West. But this was also the source of his extraordinary strength when the revolution was withdrawing into its national shell. He, who had hardly ever looked beyond that shell, found little or no difficulty in divorcing Bolshevism from the Western Marxist outlook.

His rivals had, like Lenin, lived as émigrés in Germany, France, and other European countries. There, for many years, they listened with enthusiasm to the great speeches of Jaurès and Bebel, the pioneers and prophets of French and German socialism. They absorbed the teachings of Kautsky and Guesde, the leading expounders of Marxism. They viewed with admiration and envy the scores of great socialist newspapers and journals, which were openly published and read by the million, while the Russian revolutionaries could bring out only a few small clandestine sheets, which they smuggled into Russia with much difficulty and great danger to themselves. They watched with rapture the parliamentary strength, and the political and educational institutions, of Western Marxism, the massive trade unions, the 'powerful' and openly conducted strikes, the May Day demonstrations, etc., etc. They were held spellbound by the 'might' of European Marxism.

Then came the great collapse of 1914, when, despite all the previous professions of anti-militarism and internationalism, the power of the Western parties was harnessed to the war machines of the belligerent governments. But the Russian émigrés still believed that the inherent 'class consciousness' and power of the Western proletariat would overcome this 'betrayal' and its consequences. They found it hard to shed this belief even some years after they had themselves become Russia's rulers.

Stalin had known none of their enthusiasms and none of their illusions. He had never sat at the feet of Jaurès, Bebel, Kautsky, and Guesde. He had never had any first-hand impression of the apparent might of the Marxist movement in the West. Even during the Leninist era when he too expressed hope for the spread of the revolution, he was merely adopting what was then the conventional Bolshevik idiom. When that hope was shattered, his inward balance was not upset. Unlike many old Bolsheviks, he did not feel that the Russian revolution and its makers were now suspended over an abyss. Even as early as the beginning of 1918 he had expressed icy scepticism about the revolutionary movements of the West, and brought upon his head a rebuke from Lenin. Paradoxically, Stalin's ignorance of the West led him to a more realistic appreciation of its revolutionary potentialities than that which other Bolshevik leaders, including Lenin, had reached after many years of first-hand observation and study.

The democratic orientation of the early Bolshevik leaders was also up to a point bound up with the Western Marxist tradition. Under the Tsar Bolshevism could exist and work only underground. Any underground movement, if it is to be effective, must be led in a more or less authoritarian manner. It must be strictly disciplined, hierarchically organized, and centrally controlled. Nearly all Russian revolutionary movements (and all the Resistance movements in Nazi-occupied Europe of 1940–5 as well) were characterized by such features. The chiefs of any clandestine party must exalt the idea of strict discipline and strong leadership on which survival of such a party largely depends. In his time Lenin exalted the principle of strong leadership with all the emphasis and over-emphasis peculiar to him.

Yet even the underground Bolshevik organization of Tsarist days was by no means the monolithic body the Stalinist legend depicted.

The Bolshevik émigrés had before their eyes the example of the Western labour organizations, in which free debate flourished and democratic procedures were strictly observed, even if in fact most of those organizations too were effectively controlled by centralized and self-willed caucuses. The Bolshevik emissary who, on a false passport, travelled between Western Europe and Russia, was often torn between the democratic outlook of the Western parties and the clandestine authoritarianism of his own movement. He dreamt of the day when his party too would emerge into the open, freely debate its affairs, adopt democratic procedures, and freely elect its leaders. Whenever the Bolshevik Party did emerge into the open, if only for a short spell as in 1905, Lenin did indeed infuse democracy into it. And from 1917 to 1920 inner party democracy flourished in Bolshevik ranks.

Stalin's political outlook had been formed exclusively by clandestine Bolshevism. He had been one of those disciplinarian committee-men who had jealously guarded the Bolshevik organization from infiltration by alien elements and *agents provocateurs*. In a clandestine organization the rank and file could not freely elect their leaders —often they could not even be allowed to know who the leaders were. The committee-man not unnaturally sensed in any attempt at democratization the threat of disruption and the danger of exposure to the political police.

This outlook of the old underground leader remained with Stalin throughout his lifetime. He regarded, as he himself said later, the turbulent, open debates in which the party indulged between 1917 and 1920 as a waste of time and a drain on the party's efficiency and striking power. Of course, he too had to speak occasionally, in deference to precept, about the need for inner-party democracy. But he never even began to realize that genuine freedom of criticism and the open clash of opinion might be a creative ferment keeping a party mentally alive and vigorous.

Having risen to power, he carried the habits of clandestine Bolshevism to a grotesque extreme, and transplanted them into the Soviet State and into the life of a whole nation, in which, anyhow, all democratic impulses had become atrophied.

Finally, Stalin was as if predestined to become the chief mouthpiece of Bolshevism when it was absorbing the Russian 'way of life' and the sombre heritage of the Tsarist past. In that heritage the Greek Orthodoxy was a dominant element. Stalin had imbibed it in his youth. True, many a Russian revolutionary received his education in an Orthodox Seminary, especially in the Caucasus. Nor need a revolutionary trained in his youth to be a priest preserve the theological cast of mind for the rest of his life. But Stalin did preserve it in an extraordinary degree.

Before he imposed the Greek Orthodox style and manner upon the Bolshevik Party, that style and manner had in his own mind imposed themselves upon his Marxism and atheism. He presented the Marxist and Leninist formulæ in the accent, the intonation, and sometimes even the idiom of Greek Orthodoxy, which made those formulæ sound less alien to the 'backward' Russian masses. Indeed, he made Bolshevism appear as something like a new emanation of the old and indefinable spirit of the Church, long before he rehabilitated the Church itself for reasons of expediency.

It is enough, for instance, to read Stalin's famous oath of fealty to Lenin, that strange litany which he intoned after Lenin's death and in which he began every invocation with the refrain 'We swear to Thee, Comrade Lenin', to feel with almost physical immediacy the ex-pupil of the monks, trained in the delivery of sermons and funeral orations, emerging in the disciple of Lenin and overtopping the Marxist.

This is only the most striking instance of that amalgamation of Marxism and Greek Orthodoxy which was characteristic of Stalin and Stalinism. Even in his most sophisticated writings, up to his last essay on the 'Economic Problems of Socialism in the U.S.S.R.', he gave his arguments an inimitable scholastic twist, as if he were dealing not with the realities of political power and social life but with the theological interpretation of dogma.

If the trend of the Russian revolution was towards national self-centredness, autocracy, and quasi-ecclesiastical orthodoxy, then Stalin was its ideal agent. But these political formulæ, correct in themselves, have not yet touched the innermost psychological springs of Stalinism, which may have to be sought far below political consciousness, in the imagination and the instincts of a primitive people.

The Russia of the early and middle 1920's was at an extremely low level of civilization. Barefoot and illiterate *muzhiks*, most of whom tilled their tiny plots of land with wooden ploughs, still formed the overwhelming majority of the nation. There were also the tribes of mountaineers in the Caucasus, and the nomad-shepherds and semi-nomads of the Asiatic provinces—all submerged in an even more ancient way of life.

The sheer weight of these elements was great. True enough, in the events of 1917 the industrial workers of Petrograd (Leningrad) and Moscow were the decisive actors. But their political ascendancy came to an end with the ebbing of the revolution and with the physical dispersal of the metropolitan working class during the civil wars. In the years of Stalin's rise the upsurge of rural Russia and of her Asiatic and semi-Asiatic fringes was one of the most striking features of Russian life.

Much of the thinking and imagination of rural Russia was still below the level even of Greek Orthodoxy or of any organized religious thought. It was immersed in the primitive magic of rudimentary society. We know from the investigators of the earliest phases of civilization and from the Freudists how many remnants of primitive magic may be traced in the imagination and behaviour even of modern and relatively educated nations. But we also know that primitive magic expressed man's helplessness amid the forces of nature which he had not yet

learned to control; and that, on the whole, modern technology and organization are its deadliest enemies. On the
technological level of the wooden plough primitive magic
flourishes.

Under Lenin Bolshevism had been accustomed to
appeal to the reason, the self-interest, and the enlightened
idealism of 'class-conscious' industrial workers. It spoke
the language of reason even when it appealed to the
muzhiks. But once Bolshevism had ceased to rely on
revolution in the West, once it had lost the sense of its
own elevation above its native environment, once it had
become aware that it could only fall back on that environment and dig itself in, it began to descend to the level of
primitive magic, and to appeal to the people in the
language of that magic.

In Stalin the world of primitive magic was perhaps
even more strongly alive than the tradition of Greek
Orthodoxy. In his native Georgia the tribal way of life,
with its totems and taboos, had survived into his own
day. The Caucasus had been the meeting ground of
Oriental and Greek mythologies, which had permeated
native poetry and folklore. We know even from official
Soviet biographies how strongly these worked upon the
mind of the young Stalin; and, according to all the evidence, his deeply emotional, unsophisticated sensitivity
to folk legend remained with him to the last. Quite
recently, Mr. Budu Svanidze, Stalin's nephew, has told
us what a strong hold some of the tribal Georgian taboos
had on Stalin in his mature years. Incidentally, Mr.
Svanidze, who was once his uncle's courtier and is still
his admirer, relates this with the tribesman's pride rather
than with any intention to detract from Stalin's greatness.

He dwells in particular on the fact that Stalin was
powerfully swayed by the Georgian traditions of blood
feud. He describes, for instance, a pre-revolutionary
incident when Stalin refused to sing a certain song in the
presence of two Georgian party members, because the
song was about a blood feud in which the ancestors of his

D

two comrades had been involved as enemies. When someone remarked that his scruples were ridiculous and that the
two Georgians 'were no longer savage mountaineers or
feudal princes' but members of the same revolutionary
party, 'Stalin replied: "It makes no difference. We
Georgians have our own code of a tooth for a tooth, an
eye for an eye, a life for a life—the law of the Khevsures,
which obliges us to take vengeance. Revolutionaries or
not, comrades or not, the law still binds us. No Georgian
ever forgives an offence or an insult to himself, to his
family, or to his forebears. Never!"'

Mr. Svanidze goes on to say that in the great purges
of 1936–8 Stalin was influenced once again by the traditions of 'the tribe of the Khevsures, who gave to Georgia
its basic customs, above all the law of vengeance and
vendetta'. While Stalin was brooding over the decision
to start the purges, he went to the Crimea, retired into
solitude, but took with him his nephew in order to have
by his side, again in accordance with the primordial
Georgian custom, a man of his tribe before embarking
upon the blood feud.

It is difficult to dismiss all this as petty gossip, as one
might otherwise be inclined to do, when one considers
how much of the spirit of primitive magic Stalin brought
with him into Bolshevism.

The most characteristic landmark of Stalinist Moscow,
indeed of Stalinist Russia, was the Lenin Mausoleum in
the Red Square, to which long queues of Russian
peasants and visitors from the most remote Asiatic
corners of the U.S.S.R. made their pilgrimage to see the
mummy of the founder of Bolshevism. The Mausoleum
had been set up despite the protests of Krupskaya,
Lenin's widow, and of other members of the Central
Committee. To old Bolsheviks its mere sight was an
offence to their dignity, and—so they thought—an insult
to the maturity of the Soviet people. The Mausoleum
was the monument which primitive magic erected to
itself in the very heart of the Russian revolution, the

totem pole and the shrine of Stalinism. It had its fascina-
tion for the Soviet people; it was for them a place of
pilgrimage during nearly thirty years. (And Stalin's oath
of fealty to the dead Lenin had all the undertones of a
funeral homage to a deceased tribal chief.)

Under Stalin the story of Bolshevism came to be re-
written in terms of sorcery and magic, with Lenin and
then Stalin as the chief totems.

In the tribal cults there can be no graver sin than to
offend the totem; and so in the Stalin cult whoever had
at any time disagreed or quarrelled with Lenin was guilty
of sacrilege. (Stalin himself, of course, was quite cynical
about this. He knew the real history of all the inner party
controversies; and he himself had had his disagreements
with Lenin. But this was the manner in which the story
of the party had to be presented in order to help to secure
his own immunity from criticism and attack.)

Stalin's opponents, Bukharin and others, had to be
charged with the attempt to murder the ancestral totem
—the cardinal sin in primitive magic. They were indeed
accused of having attempted to assassinate not only
Stalin but Lenin also; and the charge was brought against
them twenty years after the alleged attempt. The whole
atmosphere of the purge trials, with their countless
accusations, their incredible confessions, and all the
violent curses thrown at the defendants by prosecutors,
judges, and witnesses, can never be fully explained,
whatever the plausible political explanations, in terms
other than those of primitive magic.

And what was Stalin himself, the remote, inaccessible
ruler, the Life-giving Sun, the Father of all the two
hundred millions of Soviet citizens, if not the totem whom
the tribe considers as its forebear and with whom all the
members of the tribe must feel themselves in a close
personal relationship?

Something like a belief in the transmigration of the
political souls of great leaders was essential to the Stalin
cult: Lenin was the 'Marx of his time', Stalin was the

'Lenin of his time'. This motif too sprang from the inner recesses of the primitive imagination.

In recent years the world was taken aback by the irrational campaign designed to convince the Soviet people that the Russians, and the Russians alone, had been the initiators of all the epoch-making ideas and of all the modern technical discoveries. The campaign may have been dictated by cold political calculation, by the desire to enhance Russia's self-confidence in the conflict with the West. In respect of its claims, the campaign has by no means been unique. Almost every Western nation has at one time or another boosted itself by means of chauvinistic self-adulation. But the grotesque form which the self-adulation has assumed in Russia transcends the experience of any modern chauvinism. It goes back to that remote epoch when the tribe cultivated a belief in its own mysterious powers which set it apart from and above all other tribes.

Similarly, the fear instilled in Soviet citizens of contamination by contact with the West has been in its violence and irrationality reminiscent of the taboo—it suggests the savages' dread of incest.

Stalinism is a complex phenomenon, which needs to be viewed from many angles. But when it is seen from the angle from which we are now viewing it, it appears as the mongrel offspring of Marxism and primitive magic.

Marxism has its inner logic and consistency: and its logic is modern through and through. Primitive magic has its own integrity and its peculiar poetic beauty. But the combination of Marxism and primitive magic was bound to be as incoherent and incongruous as is Stalinism itself. Stalin was exceptionally well equipped to embody that combination and to reconcile in some degree the irreconcilables. But he did not himself create the combination. It was produced by the impact of a Marxist revolution upon a semi-Asiatic society and by the impact of that society upon the Marxist revolution.

CHAPTER FOUR

THE LEGACY OF STALINISM
I. DOMESTIC AFFAIRS

STALINISM, we have seen, was no accidental phenomenon in post-revolutionary Russia. It was no freak
of history, as some of its old-Bolshevik opponents were
inclined to believe. It had its roots deep in its native soil,
and it quite naturally flourished in its native climate.
This accounted in the last instance for its stupendous
strength and resilience, which allowed it to survive so
many convulsions and shocks that might have broken
any less organically constituted regime.

The question whether Stalinism can survive Stalin for
long depends on whether the social conditions from
which it had sprung are still prevalent in the Soviet
Union. Does the blend of Marxism, autocracy, Greek
Orthodoxy, and primitive magic still satisfy a vital need
of Russia's development? If so, then, failing some
national calamity like a defeat in war, Stalinism may be
expected to survive Stalin for a long time, regardless of
temporary difficulties and possible rivalry and division
in the ruling group. But if the social conditions which
have produced it have vanished or are about to do so,
then Stalinism cannot long endure.

A survey of the legacy of Stalinism, in both domestic
and foreign affairs, may therefore not be out of place
here. What does that legacy consist of? What meaning
has it for the present and for the new and rising Soviet
generations?

In trying to answer these questions one does not have
to resort to guesswork, but has only to draw certain

inferences from the changes which Stalinism has wrought in Soviet society.

The changes are, on the whole, well known, although the knowledge of them is no guarantee against the temptation to think of the Russia of the 1950's in terms that would have been perfectly up to date and realistic in the 1930's, or even 1940's, but which are now becoming obsolete. It is a common propensity of the political analyst to lag mentally behind the times. It is even more common for statesmen and politicians to try to apply to new problems solutions successfully or even unsuccessfully applied to previous situations. We are liable to make such errors in our thinking about any nation. But with regard to no nation is this time lag likely to be as great as in relation to Russia, because every recent decade has brought about changes in Russia's national existence more radical and profound than those normally occurring in the life of a nation over half a century.

The West has had its eyes fixed on the purges, the witch-hunts, and the terror which Stalinism employed in its merciless struggle to perpetuate its hold over the minds and bodies of the Soviet people, and more recently of all peoples within the Soviet orbit. That struggle has been real enough; and so has its effectiveness. Yet it was Stalin himself, not his opponents, who in a sense waged the most bitter and effective struggle against the perpetuation of his own system.

Stalinism has persistently and ruthlessly destroyed the soil in which it had grown, that primitive, semi-Asiatic society on whose sap it fed. By its barbarous methods it has succeeded in driving out of Russia most of the barbarism from which it had drawn its strength.

It has achieved this because, even while it expressed the ascendancy of the Oriental-Russian backwardness over Marxism, it also represented the dictatorship of Marxism over that backwardness.

Marxism had postulated an industrial society as the prerequisite for the establishment of socialism. In a titanic struggle with the inefficiency, the sluggishness, and the anarchy of Mother Russia, Stalinism has carried its industrial revolution almost to every corner of its Eurasian realm. The core of Stalin's genuine historic achievement lies in the fact that he found Russia working with the wooden plough and left her equipped with atomic piles.

None of the great nations of the West has carried out its industrial revolution in so short a time and under such crippling handicaps.

Great Britain long enjoyed the advantages of being the world's first and only industrial workshop. Protected by the Channel from foreign invasion, the British devoted their undivided economic strength to the development of their productive resources. The industrialization of Britain, now gaining and now losing momentum, stretched over centuries.

In the United States the process took several decades only. But the United States benefited from exceptional geographic, climatic, and historical advantages. Its people were protected by two oceans and had no need to waste their resources on the requirements of war. They were also fortunate in not having to break down and to overcome inherited anachronistic forms of economic life in their own country. And they were assisted by an abundant influx of foreign capital and machinery, by the immigration of many enterprising spirits and vast numbers of skilled and unskilled labour from all countries of the old world.

Germany also was assisted in her industrialization by foreign capital; and she could freely draw on resources in craftsmanship accumulated over the ages. The process by which Germany changed from an agricultural into an industrial nation lasted nearly half a century, a half-century of an expanding world economy and peace in Europe (1871–1914), which allowed Germany to invest only a negligible proportion of her resources in unproductive armaments.

The Stalinist industrial revolution has so far lasted

less than a quarter of a century; and nearly half a decade of this was taken up by a most devastating war, which obliterated much of the achievement of previous years. Even in peace the threat of war hung over Russia's vulnerable frontiers most of the time; and armament production drained off a huge portion of the nation's resources. Foreign investment played no part in Soviet industrialization. The contribution of foreign skill and labour, if not totally absent, was comparatively negligible, while Russia's own resources in administrative and industrial skill were extremely poor.

Tens of millions of *muzhiks* had to be hastily trained as industrial workers; and hundreds of thousands of men and women had to become technicians and managers within the shortest possible time. Managers and workers alike had to acquire their skill on the job like soldiers who learn to handle rifles and guns for the first time on the battle-field. The effectiveness of the industrialization was correspondingly reduced. Nor could industrialization be carried out on the scale intended without a forcible break-up of anachronistic forms of economic life, especially of the primitive small farm, which tied up labour needed in industry and which could not feed the swelling industrial population. The forcible break-up of the old rural economy engendered chaos, famine, and widespread and violent discontent which in its turn drove the industrializers to use even more violence in the pursuit of their objectives. All this again reduced the effectiveness of industrialization.

This is the economic story of Stalinism in the 1930's. Many critics have convincingly exposed the inhuman cruelties then perpetrated by Stalinism. Their criticisms have by now become so familiar and widely accepted in the West that they need not be repeated here. However, the exclusive and somewhat belated dwelling on the horrors of Stalinist industrialization tends to obscure the general balance of the Stalin era and to substitute the picture of the Russia of the 1930's for that of mid-century

Russia. Much, although by no means all, of the dust of the murderous 1930's has long since settled; and towards the end of the Stalin era the Russian scene presented a very different aspect from that of the middle of that era.

The up-to-date balance sheet of the Soviet industrial revolution can be outlined here only in the most general terms.

In the early years of the Stalin era Russia's industrial strength was hardly more than that of any small, or at the most of any medium-sized Western nation. In those days Russian economists still looked up to France, the most backward of the industrial powers of the West, while Germany was a giant whom they admired and feared. American technology was fabulously remote, as if beyond the range of the imagination.

Towards the end of the 1930's the Soviet Union, as an economic power, was catching up with and beginning to surpass Germany, as can be seen from the following basic figures:

Basic Industrial Figures for Germany* and Russia in 1929 and 1940

		1929	1940
Output of coal .. (in millions of tons)	Russia	41	166
	Germany	177	185–190
Steel .. .. (in millions of tons)	Russia	5	18
	Germany	18	20
Electricity .. .. (in billions of kwh)	Russia	6	48
	Germany	30	55
Goods traffic on railways .. .. (in millions of tons)	Russia	187	590
	Germany	463	500 (approx.)

* The figures for Germany do not include the output of Austria, the Sudetenland, and other territories annexed by Hitler.

The table indicates, of course, only that Russia's aggregate industrial power was catching up with Germany's. The degree of Russia's industrial saturation was, because of her much more numerous population, well below the German level. In consumer industries Russia was far behind Germany. On the other hand, in engineering and armament industries she was already well ahead of Germany precisely because she devoted only a negligible proportion of her basic materials to consumer industries and used them mainly for the expansion of her engineering plant.

*Basic Production**

	Million metric tons			
	U.S.S.R. in 1951	*U.S.S.R. plan for* 1955	*Great Britain, France, and West Germany* 1951	*United States* 1951
Coal ..	281	372	398	523
Oil	42	70	1·7	309
Electricity .. (billion kwh)	103	162	147	370
Pig iron ..	22	34	29	63
Crude steel	31	44	39	95

* This table is taken from *The Economist* of 30 August 1952. Another table in the same paper showed that Russia's industrial saturation, i.e. her output per head of population, remains well below that of Western Europe, although it is approaching that of France. Here again, Russia is much further behind Western Europe in consumer industries than this table indicates, but she is also more ahead in engineering and armament.

In the present decade Russia is beginning to overtake the combined industrial power of Germany, France, and

Great Britain; and she obviously aspires to catching up with the United States in the not too remote future.

Whether or not Russia will ever be able to realize her ambition of attaining industrial parity with the United States, the mere fact that she is about to leave behind the combined industrial power of the great nations of Western Europe and is thinking ahead so ambitiously, gives a measure of the profound transformation she has undergone in the Stalin era.

This transformation has taken place on the basis of a publicly owned and planned economy. Stalinism claims to have provided the first historically significant demonstration, carried out on a gigantic scale, that planning is the most effective method for the rational use and the most rapid development of a nation's economic resources. Stalinism has implanted this conviction in the new Soviet generations even in its most bitter opponents and enemies among them; and it impresses upon the new generations of China and Eastern Europe that their way of escape from inherited poverty and the anarchy of their underdeveloped capitalism lies also in a publicly owned and planned economy.

What validity, it may be asked, has this claim concerning the superiority of Soviet planning? How much of Russia's industrial expansion has been due to planning, and how much has been achieved by, for instance, the use of forced labour?

It is important to make a distinction between the fundamental elements of the Soviet economy and its marginal phenomena. A few years ago the number of the inmates of Soviet concentration camps was most implausibly estimated by Western commentators from 12 to 20 millions. If these figures were correct the whole Soviet experiment in planning would be only of negative significance to the rest of the world, for it would represent nothing but the recrudescence of slavery on a staggering scale.

However, much laborious research and some evidence from inside Russia have reduced these speculative figures to more plausible proportions. Dr. N. M. Jasny for instance, an able but also a most extreme Menshevik critic of Stalinist economic policies, has reached the conclusion that at the height of the deportations the total number of inmates of those camps may have amounted to three or four millions. Morally, this makes little difference: the use of forced labour is equally repugnant and its condemnation remains equally valid whether four or twenty million people are involved. But a more precise idea of the dimensions of the problem helps to bring the economic picture of the Stalin era into more realistic focus. It disposes of the theory that the Soviet economy could not function without forced labour.

In an economy in which the total number of workers and employees is about 40 millions—it was over 30 millions before the Second World War—and in which further scores of millions work on collective farms, the labour of four million convicts is a marginal factor. The brunt of the industrialization has been borne by a working class which has been severely regimented, disciplined, and directed, but which is essentially a normal working class.

The impressive results of Stalinist planning should not cause incredulous surprise in the West. After all, the West, too, has learned from its own experience about the advantages of planning, even though it has so far planned its economic resources and activities only sporadically, and under the stress of war. It is enough to glance at the industrial statistics of the United States and of Great Britain to realize that in this century both these nations developed their industries at an incomparably faster rate during the few war years, when they adopted some elements of planning, than during whole decades of uncontrolled economy in peace. In both countries the economic story of the two inter-war decades (1919–39) is one of overall stagnation compared with the great expansion of 1940–4.

According to the *Federal Reserve Bulletin* (February 1953, p. 161) the overall index of American industrial production, taking the level of output in 1935–9 as 100, oscillated around this level for two decades, declining steeply in years of depression and rising only slightly above it in years of prosperity and reaching the highest point, 113, in 1937. It took the Second World War and some planning to send the index of production soaring to 239 in 1943.

Is it to be wondered at that Russia's comprehensive planning over a quarter of a century has shown cumulative effects? True, even Russia's top planners had to train themselves on their jobs. They committed many monstrous mistakes, for which the nation and the State had to pay. But they also gradually accumulated experience and perfected the technique of planning. In recent years their work has consequently shown much more self-confidence and efficiency than it did in the 1930's.

The test came after the cease-fire of 1945, when Russia's wealthiest (western and southern) provinces lay in ruins, their cities razed, their coal-mines flooded, and their factories demolished. Within four or five years the Russian economy staged a remarkable recovery. How this has affected Russia's power-political position can be seen from the fact that in the opening phase of the cold war Russia's annual output of steel was only one-eighth or one-seventh of America's. It is at present well over one-third; and it is planned to be nearly one-half of the American output by the middle of the 1950's.

It is time to consider how these economic changes have affected the social climate of Russia.

The Stalin era has been one of rapid urbanization. In the last pre-war decade alone the Soviet town population increased by 30 millions, of whom no fewer than 25 millions were peasants shifted from country to town, a fact which helps to explain the notoriously abominable housing conditions in Soviet cities. Even during the last war a multitude of new towns sprang up in the Asiatic provinces, towns the location of which is not even indicated on ordinary Russian maps. Urbanization was resumed after the war and is still going on, although, naturally, its momentum has slowed down.[1]

The millions of *muzhiks* turned into modern industrial workers had to be taught to read and write, to handle precision tools, and to understand something of complicated technological processes. They had also to be broken in to the regular industrial rhythm of life; and they had to acquire within a few years the habits of industrial discipline which the West had inculcated into its working classes, by coercion and persuasion, over the centuries.

What this meant will become clearer if it is remembered that the life of Russia's rural population had been entirely regulated by the rhythm of nature, and by a most severe climate. The *muzhik* had been accustomed to work from sunrise to sunset in the summer and to sleep through most of the winter. A most rigorous, inhuman factory discipline was used to break him of these habits. But towards the end of the 1930's the new discipline had been more or less achieved; and in the closing years of the Stalin era the Soviet Union already had a vast trained, modern labour force, which could be expanded in a less revolutionary and violent manner. The most baffling and cruel job was to accumulate a national fund of industrial knowledge and know how—the accretions were then bound to come more organically and easily. The rapid formation from the rawest human

[1] The present Soviet town population is estimated at 70 millions, nearly 45 millions more than at the beginning of the Stalin era.

material of this industrial labour force was the most essential part of the so-called cultural revolution of Stalinism.

Technology, planning, urbanization, and industrial expansion are the deadliest enemies of the primitive magic of Stalinism. Russia's rulers could not teach with impunity chemistry, physics, mathematics, medicine, and the use of industrial tools to the children of semi-illiterate workers, wholly illiterate *muzhiks*, and nomads and shepherds. The rulers themselves made an anachronism of the Stalin cult. They dragged the mind of Russia out of the epoch of the wooden plough and of primitive myth into the world of science and industry; and now they cannot expect it to feel at ease in the stuffy air of the Stalin cult and to accept uncritically its antics.

For social, political, and strategic reasons, Stalinism has carried the industrial revolution beyond the Urals to the Asiatic lands, to the very homeland of primitive magic. There fifty or so per cent of Soviet basic industry and engineering plant is now concentrated. There Soviet Chicagos, Pittsburghs, and Detroits have sprung up in an environment which even in this generation was not much different from the cultural level of the Red Indian communities of early America. The primitive element is still being dissolved, sucked in, and digested by the centres of a fresh and vital industrial civilization. Can one assume for a moment that all this will have no effect on Russia's political mentality?

Modernization has not been confined to the urban population. The town has strongly reacted upon the country. The thirty or forty millions who had migrated or been shifted to the towns during the Stalin era did not lose all contact with their earlier environment. They have been the human channels through which modern civilization has infused itself into the life of rural Russia.

The infusion has been all the more effective because of the simultaneous revolution in the technology of farming and in the social framework of rural life. On the fields the tractor, the combine-harvester, and the lorry have replaced the horse and the ox. The old smallholder, with his conservative self-sufficiency and indifference to the great issues of the age, has given place to the collective farmer, the member of an intricate and interdependent community which is more and more acutely aware of its own dependence on governmental policy, on developments in industry, and on the state of international affairs.

Here again, Stalinism in its very struggle for life and power was committing suicide by slow degrees. At the start collectivization gave Stalinism effective control over the peasantry. However, historically the omnipotence of the centralist Russian bureaucracy was based on the political impotence of an atomized peasantry. As long as the bulk of the nation existed in a politically amorphous state and was inherently incapable of self-organization, the absolute government at the centre enjoyed unrestricted freedom of movement, except at times when it was threatened by urban revolution. In collectivization, as Stalin himself once remarked, there lurks a threat to any centralist bureaucracy, because collectivization concentrates the peasantry's scattered strength and imparts to it a much greater potential power in politics than it had before.

Contemplation of the atrocious methods by which collectivization had been forced on the peasantry should not obscure the fact that with the years the basic structure of collective farming became consolidated and stabilized. In those far-off days of 1929–33, when the party sent out its shock brigades to collectivize the *muzhiks'* land and cattle, the *muzhiks* thought that this was the end of the world, as indeed it was for those among them who fiercely resisted and were made to suffer for it. Since then the bulk of the peasantry has somehow adjusted itself to the collectivist framework of its existence and has also found within it some scope for the satisfaction of private interests.

The productivity of Soviet farming and the farmers' standard of living have been rising in recent years. What may surprise us is not that this should happen but that it should happen so late, and that the rise should be so slow.

Under the Five Year Plans the government lavishly invested in agriculture, saturating it with machinery, tractors, combine-harvesters, artificial fertilizers, and so on. The State also trained agronomists, accountants, and administrators *en masse*. More recently it embarked upon ambitious schemes for afforestation and irrigation which should increase the fertility of the soil and protect it from recurrent droughts. In relation to all these efforts the rise in the output of Soviet farming has been modest; and it has lagged behind the growth of the industrial population.[1]

There were plenty of reasons why collectivization and mechanization should bear fruit only slowly. Throughout most of the 1930's the effectiveness of mechanization was nearly nullified by the technological backwardness and the political restiveness of the peasantry. The *muzhik* was either incapable of handling the new machines or, resenting collectivization, deliberately damaged and broke them as the Luddites had done in an earlier age. Only in the late 1930's did the unrest subside enough and the handling of the machines improve sufficiently to make an advance possible. This was soon interrupted by the war, which deprived farming of its manpower and disrupted and depleted its technical equipment. The first post-war Plan (1946–50) was largely devoted to re-equipment. Only in the early 1950's could agriculture resume the advance it had begun fifteen years before.

[1] Students of Soviet agriculture disagree about the extent of the rise in its output. The most extreme critics put it at 20 per cent higher than before collectivization. The official Soviet figure is over 40 per cent. Whatever the truth, the present output is attained with much less agricultural labour; and so output per man-year has risen much more steeply.

E

Collective farming has thus enjoyed only two very brief spells of the social, political, and technological stability which it needed in order to show that it could be much more efficient and of greater advantage to the peasants than the primitive smallholding. The recent rise in agricultural output may therefore be regarded as the first delayed dividend on national investment in farming and on educational progress. Much greater returns ought probably to be expected. Collective farming has still to prove its worth; but if a new war or domestic convulsions do not upset its work, it should be able to do so in the near future with most beneficial effects upon the national standard of living.

This is not to say that collective farming really presents such a picture of perfect socialist harmony as is painted by Stalinist propaganda. The more enlightened the collective farmer the greater is his self-assurance, and the less is he likely to put up with the incompetent and arbitrary meddling of a bureaucracy. Soviet newspapers have in their muted manner given recently a number of indications of friction between the collective farmer and the bureaucratic bully. The tug-of-war is likely to grow more intense in consequence not of the peasants' poverty and sullenness but of their growing well-being and self-confidence.

Nor has the perennial clash of interests between town and country been finally resolved. It has only been kept within bounds; and it is now passing on to 'a higher level', as Stalin himself indicated in his last published essay on economics.

The outlook of the town is determined by public ownership and planning. In agriculture, on the other hand, a precarious balance between public and private interest has so far operated; and agriculture has up to a point retained a market economy. Planning and market relations are antagonistic to each other.

In the long run, as Stalin argued, the planned sector of the economy will strive to eliminate the rural market and to embrace farming as well. The collective farms, in which 'group ownership' is still dominant (as it is in any co-operative enterprise), would eventually become national property, in one form or another. In his last essay and correspondence Stalin sketched something like a long-term plan of agricultural policy pointing in this direction. He insisted that the transition should be carried out gradually and slowly so as not to antagonize the peasants. It remains to be seen whether it can or will be effected in the mild, evolutionary manner or whether it will lead to new violent conflicts between State and peasantry.

Whatever the prospects, industrialization, collectivization, modernization, and planning are enduring elements in the domestic balance of the Stalin era.

As Russia looks back, with pride or resentment, upon the road which she has travelled in blood, toil, and sweat during these last decades, she must know in her heart that there is no way back for her from the stage of development she has reached.

There is no way back from industrialization.

In this respect Russia is sharing the fate of older industrial nations, who have not been able to conjure out of existence the tremendous productive forces they have brought to life. The Cervanteses of the industrial age, for instance Tolstoy in Russia and Ruskin in England, have mourned the chivalries of faded epochs, depicted the curses of science and technology, and implored mankind to retrace its steps and recapture the beauty and integrity of a primitive, 'natural' way of life. But mankind, even if it listened with forebodings to their warnings and injunctions, could not retrace its steps.

Chicago cannot again become the idyllic little market town of the farmers of Illinois, which the late John Dewey still saw in his young days and described wistfully to the author shortly before his death. No more can Chkalov, Malenkov's home-town, or Sverdlovsk (in the Urals), with their giant engineering plants and power stations, change back, the first into the dreamy meeting place of the Orenburg Cossacks and the second into the fur traders' market-place of old.

Industrialization is now for Russia a matter not merely of national pride and ambition but of physical survival. In a country where the State employs over 40 million people in its industries and administrative establishments, and where even the functioning of mechanized agriculture depends entirely on the nation's mines, steel mills, engineering plant, and means of transport, any serious hitch or halt in industrial development, not to speak of de-industrialization, would bring unemployment and starvation to scores of millions. In telling the Soviet people that it alone of all conceivable Russian parties and groups stood for the programme of industrialization, Stalinism succeeded in identifying itself in the eyes of the people with their most vital interests. It derived further strength from telling them that in case of war the West would aim at 'reducing the Soviet Union to colonial status', that is at obliterating the industrial achievements of the Stalin era.

As it will be argued later, there may be ample room for certain shifts of emphasis in the programmes of industrialization. But it cannot be expected that post-Stalinist Russia will renounce this part of Stalin's legacy.

There is no way back from collective farming either.

We cannot know with certainty whether or not the great majority of Soviet peasants are inwardly reconciled to the collectivist system. All the old Russian émigrés and many vocal recent refugees from the Soviet Union take it for granted that the peasants are still longing to return to the old smallholdings, and are only awaiting the opportunity. Though there is some evidence to support this view, against it must be set the fact that collective farming withstood the shock of the last war much better than might have been expected; and that it did not show any serious signs of a break-up. Nor does it seem probable that the younger generation of peasants brought up under the new system is really hankering to return to small-scale private farming.

But even if it were assumed that the peasants are still full of nostalgia for the pre-collectivist economic system, they are no more free to go back to it than the mass of workers in Ford's factories are to become small, independent artisans.

At the beginning of the Stalin era the peasants were kept within the collective farms primarily by political force. At its end they are kept within them primarily by the force of economic circumstances, especially by the nature of the technological processes established in agriculture. A collective farm can now no more be broken up into a hundred smallholdings than a great modern liner can be broken up into small sailing boats.

If the present system of farming were to disintegrate, this would be the death sentence to innumerable human beings, town-dwellers and peasants alike. Even if a large section of the peasantry were still bent on demolishing the collectivist structure, there is no reason to suppose that Russia, under whatever regime, would allow this sectional interest to drive her to commit national suicide.

A similar view has recently been taken by so well-known and extreme a critic of Soviet agricultural policy as Dr. N. M. Jasny, quoted before. While in Dr. Jasny the anti-Soviet emotionalist is sometimes at loggerheads with the scholar, he nevertheless argues from a thorough knowledge of Soviet agriculture. In the January 1953 issue of the *Sotsialisticheskii Vestnik* he published an essay which was a *cri de cœur* against those 'irresponsible' Russian émigré politicians who 'promise' the peasants that, after the overthrow of the Soviet regime, they will abolish the collective farms.

Dr. Jasny argues that if Russian farming were to go back to the pre-collectivization system 'it could feed barely half the present urban population. Consequently a simple return to those forms would be equivalent to a huge calamity.' He also argues that if the anti-Bolsheviks were to assume power, they would have to re-enforce the compulsory food deliveries introduced by Stalin in order to prevent starvation in the towns. 'What will the Russian people eat after the overthrow of the Soviet regime and in what will they be clad?' It is enough to pose this question, says Dr. Jasny, to see the complete unreality of promising the peasants 'a free choice of the forms of farming'.

He concludes: 'I think that the preservation of the collective farms is inevitable for an indefinite time, for, in the event of their abolition, the situation after liberation from Stalinist rule, which will be difficult enough anyhow, will amount to a most enormous catastrophe.'

It is easy to see why Russian anti-Bolshevik politicians are loath to accept this view. If they did accept it, they could in effect only promise the Russian peasants that they would virtually continue the agricultural regime established by Stalin. In this instance Dr. Jasny, however, argues from realities, not from the hallucinations of political quixotry. He analyses the technological structure of Soviet farming to prove that it does not permit any break-up into smallholdings.

Most of the Soviet tractors are of the 'Leviathan' type, larger than any known outside Russia and useful only on giant farms. This type of machine, says Dr. Jasny, could be replaced by smaller ones in the course of many years (and with the help of American lend-lease deliveries!) so as to allow for a break-up of the present collective farms into smaller (but still collective) farms. But if the choice is to be only between smaller and larger *collective* farms, and if even this choice may become available only after a re-equipment taking many years, then the mountain of the anti-Stalinist 'revolution' in farming would give birth to no more than a mouse. All the same, the argument serves to underline the fact that Russia cannot afford to renounce even collectivization, that once most hateful and still most controversial part of the legacy of the Stalin era.

Nor is there any way back for Russia from public ownership and planning.

Even in capitalist countries there seems to have been not a single significant instance of any sector of the economy which had *long* been publicly owned and publicly managed being handed back to private hands.[1]

The whole of Soviet industry has been built up by the State. No title of private ownership has ever attached to it (except for the negligible remnant of pre-revolutionary industry, which has also been completely re-equipped by the State).

This fact has sunk deeply into the mind of the Russian people. Any form of private ownership in industry is to them an anachronism as repugnant and irrational as slavery or serfdom is to the British or the American peoples.

Of this we have incontrovertible evidence: among the many political groups formed in the West by the new Soviet refugees, each of which swears to destroy the whole structure of Stalinism to its very foundations, none has dared to write into its programme the abolition of public ownership of industry. On the contrary, each group ardently swears to preserve it. If this is the mood among émigrés, among the victims and the extreme opponents of Stalinism, it can be imagined how strong the attachment to public ownership is among the people in the Soviet Union.[2]

---

[1] The 're-privatization' of the British steel industry under Mr. Churchill's government has no bearing on the argument, because that industry had been nationalized *de jure* rather than *de facto* only just before the Conservative Party returned to office.

[2] In 1945–6 the author, then a correspondent for British newspapers in Germany, interviewed on this subject hundreds of Soviet 'displaced persons'. He did not meet a single person among them who reacted otherwise than with amazed indignation to the mere suggestion that public ownership might be replaced by private enterprise in Russia. Only citizens of the countries annexed by Russia in 1939–40 met the suggestion with divided opinions and most often with indifference.

With public ownership goes planning—indeed, it is inseparable from it. Even the most old-fashioned industrialist 'plans' the work of his own business. Trusts and syndicates plan and co-ordinate the productive processes within the concerns under their control. Public ownership *ipso facto* makes of the whole national industry a single concern which cannot be run without comprehensive planning. The method may undergo many important modifications. It may be more or less bureaucratic, more or less centralist, or more or less elastic and efficient; but for Russia to abandon planning would be to condemn herself to economic anarchy and ruin.

Such is the legacy of the Stalin era that posterity can neither scrap it nor get away from it. Therein consisted the greatness of that era. Yet such was also its misery and squalor that in order to make proper use of its enduring achievements, the Soviet people will be compelled sooner or later to transcend Stalinism.

Stalinism had its roots in the backwardness of Russia; but it has overcome the backwardness and has thereby potentially disestablished itself. For a time it may continue to haunt the Russia of its own making as a ghost from the past. The 'ghost' still wields all the material instruments of power; and no one can say how and when it will relinquish them or, alternatively, who will wrest them from its hands, and when. This is not a forecast of startling events, but merely a statement of the fact that a profound contradiction is maturing between, to use the Marxian term, the social and economic structure and the political superstructure of post-Stalinist society.

In the analysis of any long-term historical trend, contemporaries, even if they grasp correctly its general direction, can never be sure just how far the trend has gone at any particular time. We have no yardstick by which to measure history's molecular processes nor can we determine when those processes may coalesce to produce an epoch-making event. In the case of Russia, the measuring is the more difficult because we can know only the broad outline of the trend and we have had little or no insight into the molecular processes.

During a quarter of a century Stalinism, without compunction or pity and yet with some suppressed compassion, drove a nation of 160–200 millions to jump the chasm which separated the epoch of the wooden plough from that of the atomic pile. The jump is not yet completed. We cannot count the myriads which have landed on the farther side or those still left behind—or, even, those who have been made to jump to their destruction.

All we know is that the process is in a very advanced stage. Russia may still be mired up to her ankles or to her knees in the epoch of primitive magic; but she is not plunged in it up to her neck and ears, as she was a quarter of a century ago.

CHAPTER FIVE

THE LEGACY OF STALINISM
II. FOREIGN AFFAIRS

THE contrast between the beginning and the close of the Stalin era is equally striking when we consider Russia's attitude towards the world and her foreign policy during that period.

It will be remembered that by the middle of the 1920's the Bolshevik mind had become profoundly disturbed by the isolation of the Russian revolution. It then began to reconcile and to adapt itself to isolation, and even to glory in it. This mood found its apotheosis in the slogan 'socialism in one country', the dogma with which Stalin proclaimed the self-sufficiency and self-containment of the Russian revolution. Henceforth, adherence to this dogma became the test of loyalty to Bolshevism. Any deviation from it was branded as treason; and those who represented the revolutionary internationalism of earlier days were marked as apostates.

The halcyon days of 'socialism in one country' lasted until the Second World War.

Throughout the late 1920's and 1930's Stalin's diplomacy sought, implicitly or explicitly, to preserve the international *status quo* and to enhance Russia's position within it. 'We do not want a single square yard of foreign land' was the maxim of Chicherin and Litvinov, the two Foreign Ministers of the time.

'Not a square yard of foreign land' might also be said to have been the watchword inspiring the Communist International, which continued to claim, however, that no land on the globe was foreign to it.

The main purpose of the Stalinized Comintern was to do political guard duty for the 'only proletarian State' so that the building of socialism in 'one-sixth of the earth's territory' should not be disturbed by capitalist pressure or—by revolutionary developments in the remaining five-sixths, which might interrupt the Soviet Union's 'peaceful coexistence' with capitalism.

The Communist Parties refrained from moves which might have embarrassed Soviet diplomacy in its dealings with foreign governments. They backed all and every one of Stalin's diplomatic manœuvres either indirectly by exercising pressure upon the bourgeois governments, or directly by lending open support to the successive manœuvres on the ground that no matter how contradictory these might be, they also expressed the quintessence of international proletarian interest. It was no longer Bolshevik Russia which waited for world revolution— world revolution now had to wait until Russia had built up her socialism.

The records of the Stalinized Comintern are, of course, full of fantastic battle-cries, wild forecasts of imminent world revolution, and the most rabid upbraiding of all bourgeois and Social Democratic Parties. The records also speak of some 'putschist' incidents, stray forays in insurrectionist tactics, and displays of pseudo-revolutionary trigger-happiness. It is enough to recall here the Canton rising of 1927, or the bombastic resolutions of the Sixth Congress of the Comintern (1928), which instructed all member parties to direct their fire primarily against the social democrats in preparation for an imminent assault on the bastions of world capitalism.

However, these diversions did not affect the main trend of Soviet and Comintern policy. The communist following could not be kept inactive for an indefinite time without a consequent breakdown in its morale. When the General Staff would not allow it to engage in genuine fighting, it had to permit at least some mock battles. The need for these was the more pressing the more the communist ranks became aware that they were ordered either to render yeoman service to 'class enemies' or merely to mark time. The 'ultra-left' turns of the Comintern came, as a rule, after spells of 'rightism', which had usually left the aftertaste of self-abasement in the mouths of the rank and file.

But whenever Soviet diplomacy was engaged in serious dealings with foreign powers, the Comintern always sounded the cease-fire to its mock battles and switched back to rightist, 'opportunist' policies in which it sometimes persisted with suicidal consequences. This was true of the Communist Party of China in 1925–7; on Stalin's orders, it remained subservient to the Kuomintang up to the moment when Chiang Kai-shek ordered a massacre of the communists, and even during the massacre itself. This was also true of the French and Spanish Communist Parties during the Popular Fronts of 1936–8, when the policy of 'collective security' and of the anti-Hitler alliance with the West demanded that the radicalism of the rank and file in the Popular Fronts be kept in check. Then, in the period of the Ribbentrop-Molotov agreement (1939–41), the Comintern sought to gain acceptance of that agreement by the world's working classes by telling them that not the Third Reich but France and Britain were their chief enemies. At the next turn the Comintern became the mouthpiece of the anti-Fascist Grand Alliance, until Stalin, anxious to prove his reliability to Churchill and Roosevelt, rose up early one morning, in April 1943, and 'clave the wood for a burnt offering'. Unlike the Biblical Isaac on the way to Moriah, the Comintern did not even ask 'Where is the lamb for the burnt offering?'

Was Stalin then the great saboteur and betrayer of world revolution, as Trotsky saw him?

Yes and no. He certainly did his best to destroy the potentialities for revolution abroad—in the name of the sacred egoism of the Russian revolution. But how real and important were those potentialities between the two world wars? Trotsky saw that period as one sequence of great but missed revolutionary opportunities. The historian of the period cannot be so sure about its latent possibilities. He can gauge only its actuality, not its potentiality.

Stalin worked on the assumption that there was no chance of a communist victory in the West or in the East. If that was so, then he was sacrificing to the selfishness of Bolshevik Russia the shadow, not the substance, of world revolution. He believed that by building up the Soviet 'citadel of socialism' he was making the only contribution towards world revolution which could be made at the time. This conviction allowed him to treat the labour movements of the world with boundless cynicism and contempt.

He hoped that 'socialism in one country' would be his life's work and his party's philosophy for a whole historical epoch.

That epoch came to an end much earlier than he expected. It was brought to a close by the Second World War and its aftermath, in which the dynamics of the Soviet State and the genuine social ferment in the world combined to open a new and momentous chapter of revolution.

Conservative minds in the West have seen in Stalin the evil plotter responsible for all the revolutions of our day, because to the conservative mind revolution is always the result of plotting and conspiracy. The impartial historian will take a somewhat more complex view of this chapter in Stalin's career. He will record that in the last decade of his life Stalin struggled desperately and unavailingly to save his policy of self-containment, or what remained of it, from the tempest of the time.

He was guided by motives of orthodox strategy, not of international revolution, when, in 1939–40, he sent his armies to the Baltic lands and to the Ukrainian and Byelorussian marches of Poland. He sought to deny to Hitler these jumping-off grounds for an attack on Russia.

He could not and would not risk leaving the tiny Baltic States as independent buffers between his and Hitler's war machines. He had to incorporate them in the Soviet Union—or else, he was convinced, they would be absorbed by Greater Germany. But the Soviet Union could not effectively absorb those countries without bringing their regimes into line with its own. So Stalin's armoured brigades rolled to the Baltic coast and to the River Bug to occupy strategic outposts; but they carried revolution in the turrets of their tanks.

Even then Stalin produced the Tsars' title deeds to the annexed lands and claimed to have collected for Russia merely her old patrimony. He was still anxious to intimate that this departure from self-containment was only incidental and local in character; and that it had been dictated by national-Russian, not by international-revolutionary motives.

Then he reverted to self-containment. This was the basis of his war-time co-operation with Roosevelt and Churchill. Soviet self-containment was the very premiss of joint allied policy, written into the paragraphs and clauses of the Teheran, Yalta, and Potsdam agreements.

However, those agreements also divided spheres of influence between the Allies; and the whole of Eastern and much of Central Europe was allotted to victorious Russia. It was stipulated that this was to be the sphere of influence of Russia, not of communism. In retrospect, it appears extraordinarily shortsighted of the great states-men of the West to have believed that Russia's per-sonality could be thus split and her national-power ambi-tions separated from her social and political outlook. But the illusion was not merely Roosevelt's and Churchill's. It was shared by Stalin.

It may, of course, be argued that Stalin's behaviour during the war was nothing but make-believe, and that all his solemn vows of non-interference in the internal affairs of neighbouring countries were dust thrown into the eyes of his allies. On the other hand, Stalin's deeds at the time lent weight to his vows. Had this not been so, how is one to account for the strange circumstance that Churchill, the inspirer of the anti-Bolshevik crusade of 1918–20 and the future author of the Fulton speech, could say in the House of Commons as late as towards the end of 1944:

'Marshal Stalin and the Soviet leaders wish to live in honourable friendship and equality with the Western democracies. . . . I feel also that their word is their bond. I know of no government which stands to its obligations even in its own despite, more solidly than the Russian Soviet Government. I decline absolutely to embark here on a discussion about Russian good faith.'

The point is that both Churchill and Roosevelt had solid evidence that Stalin's policy was in fact geared to self-containment. They saw Stalin acting, not merely speaking, as any nationalist Russian statesman would have done in his place—they saw him divested, as it were, of his communist character. He was approaching the problems of the Russian zone of influence in a manner calculated to satisfy nationalist Russian demands and aspirations and to wreck the chances of communist revolution in those territories.

He prepared to exact and did in fact exact heavy reparations from Hungary, Bulgaria, Rumania, Finland, and Eastern Germany. This, he knew, would make the name of communism as well as that of Russia odious to the peoples of those countries, to whom it did not even occur to distinguish between the two. With a zeal worthy of a better cause he insisted on slicing territories away from Poland, Hungary, and Germany, and on expelling many millions of their citizens from their homes.

From Stalin's viewpoint these policies made sense only if he assumed that in all those countries bourgeois regimes would survive, that is if he had no design to impose communist governments on them. If he had been viewing those countries as future provinces of his empire, it would have been the height of folly on his part to insist on levying in the most unrelenting manner heavy reparations and enforcing expulsions. He expected, of course, that victorious Russia would enjoy a position of diplomatic and economic preponderance in neighbouring countries ruled by 'friendly governments', to quote the insipid cliché then fashionable. But he also expected that those governments would remain essentially bourgeois.

The fact which emerges with equal clarity from the internal evidence of Stalin's own moves and from the numerous memoirs of Western statesmen is that Stalin gravely underrated the revolutionary ferment which was to engulf Europe and Asia towards the end of the war and after. In his calculations he either made no allowance for it or, if he did, he took it for granted that through his Communist Parties he would be able to master and calm the ferment. He looked at the post-1945 world through the prism of the pre-1939 era.

The state of the world in the decades between the wars had convinced him that he had been right all along in discounting or disregarding the revolutionary potentialities of foreign communism; and he continued to disregard them. He saw every foreign nation as a bulwark of social and political conservatism. He tried to persuade Roosevelt that the overwhelming majority of the French were loyal to Pétain. 'Communism would fit Germany as a saddle fits a cow'—in this mordant phrase he expressed his view of Germany's revolutionary potentialities to the Polish politician Mikolajczyk. He urged the French communists to take their cue from General de Gaulle at a time when they were the chief driving force behind the French Resistance. He urged the Italian communists to make peace with the House of Savoy and with the government of Marshal Badoglio, and to vote for the re-enactment of Mussolini's Lateran pacts with the Vatican. He did his best to induce Mao Tse-tung to come to terms with Chiang Kai-shek, because he believed, as he said at Potsdam, that the Kuomintang was the only force capable of ruling China. He angrily remonstrated with Tito because of the latter's revolutionary aspirations, and demanded his consent to the restoration of the monarchy in Yugoslavia.

Nothing could sum up Stalin's mood better than this war-time dialogue with Tito:

'Be careful, [says Stalin] the bourgeoisie in Serbia is very strong!'

'Comrade Stalin, [says Tito] I do not agree. . . . The bourgeoisie in Serbia is very weak.'

'The bourgeoisie is very strong!' not only in Serbia but in China, Poland, Rumania, France, Italy—everywhere! This might have been the pivot of Stalin's policies.

He stared with incredulity and fear at the rising tides of revolution which threatened to wash away the rock of 'socialism in one country', on which he had built his temple. This so-called prophet of Marxism and Leninism appears at this moment as the most conservative statesman in the world.

He was still confident that he could stem the rising tides—he still wielded the magic wand which made these tides ebb and flow. It did not occur to him that the magic wand might break in his hands and that its fragments might soon be tossing about on the currents and cross-currents of contemporary history.

How Stalinist self-containment was subsequently wrecked, partly by forces beyond Stalin's control and partly by Stalin himself, is a complex story which can be only briefly summarized here.

The Yugoslav revolution inflicted the first telling blow on Stalin's policy. In the Teheran-Yalta period Yugoslavia had not been allotted to the Soviet sphere of influence—it was to have been a border zone between the British and the Russian spheres. Stalin was therefore doubly anxious to keep in check the revolutionary forces of Yugoslavia, whose ascendancy threatened to compromise his relations with the Western Allies. For long

F

he disparaged Tito's partisans and extolled the counter-revolutionary Chetniks of Drazha Mikhailovich as the alleged heroes of anti-Nazi resistance. The embittered Tito, still one of the most faithful agents of the Stalinist Comintern, implored him: 'If you cannot send us assistance, then at least do not hamper us.' Stalin, so Tito relates, 'stamped with rage' and tried to induce Tito to agree not merely to the restoration of the monarchy but to a possible British occupation of Yugoslavia, which would have secured the monarchy's survival. Then, at Yalta, he forced Tito into a coalition with the men of the old regime, a decision which, according to Tito, 'provoked the deepest indignation among the supporters of the National Liberation Movement in Yugoslavia'. Tito's unruly revolutionary moves were to Stalin a 'stab in the back of the Soviet Union'.[1]

Stalin's 'rage' and 'anger' can easily be understood. It came to him as a shock that he was beginning to lose control over the revolutionary ferment and even over his own Communist Parties. He had been confident that he could at any time use them as pawns in his great diplomatic game of chess. The pawns were now showing a life of their own and beginning to play their own game. The great chess master, confounded and furious, could not even lay hands on them. For one thing, the Communist Parties concerned were not always within his reach. For another, he had to save his reputation as the friend, inspirer, and leader of world communism—he could not afford the odium of an open betrayal. He had to yield to the will of the pawns and then pretend that it was he who moved them.

This inevitably produced deep cracks in the Grand Alliance. Was it perhaps after all Stalin who was moving the pawns? Roosevelt and Churchill began to wonder; and they prepared and made their own counter-moves. Was it perhaps Stalin after all? we may still ask. Even now, eight or nine years later, it is still impossible to say

[1] *Tito Speaks*, by V. Dedijer.

exactly what happened in each particular case. The 'accident' of Tito's break with Moscow has brought to light a few significant episodes in Stalin's struggle to preserve self-containment, which might otherwise have remained hidden in the archives for a long time to come. How many such incidents relating to other East European countries still remain hidden?

What is certain is that as Stalin began reluctantly to identify himself with the rising forces of foreign communism his Western allies also began to identify him with those forces. The Grand Alliance was giving place to the Great Enmity. Stalin then sought reinsurance against the West; and communist regimes in the Russian sphere of influence promised to provide it. And then it was without a doubt he who moved the pawns.[1]

This departure from self-containment was caused, however, not only by the new international tension but also by the latent forces of revolutionary dynamics within the Soviet Union. The Grand Alliance had kept those forces in check; the break-up of the Alliance released them.

The urge to carry revolution abroad 'on the bayonet points' is alive in any revolutionary State which has been compelled first to defend itself against a foreign aggressor and then to send its armies to conquer the aggressor's lands and dominions. In Napoleon's France the urge was even stronger than in Stalin's Russia. In both cases armies raised in the climate of revolution came to dominate and administer countries where the *ancien régime* was still intact. At home, officers and men had been taught to abhor the ruling classes, the institutions, and the customs and habits of the *ancien régime*. Then they were ordered to meet with obliging smiles the same old ruling classes in the conquered lands, to supervise with impartial detachment the working of their institu-

[1] According to Tito, Stalin finally decided to bring Eastern Europe under close Soviet control in 1947, at the time when the Truman doctrine was proclaimed.

tions, and to adjust themselves to alien customs and habits. This was an almost impossible demand.

Stalin's generals and colonels had from their earliest years imbibed hatred and contempt of capitalist enterprise; they had been taught to consider bourgeois and Social Democratic Parties as implacable enemies; and had been conditioned to think and act within the framework of a single party system. Is it to be wondered at that as Military Governors of Saxony, Brandenburg, Hungary, Bulgaria, and Rumania they were little inclined to administer these countries in such a way as to allow capitalist business to function as usual and non-Communist Parties, whose leaders did not even conceal their hatred and contempt of the communist conquerors, to carry on their activities without hindrance?

From the beginning, the Soviet Military Governors were caught up in a conflict between their own ingrained beliefs and their new duties. They could not sincerely carry out these duties without betraying their upbringing and outlook, or even without becoming disloyal to their own government, as some of them did. If they were to remain loyal Stalinists, they had to treat the demand of 'non-interference in domestic affairs' as mere make-believe. It would have been miraculous if they had managed to adjust their own minds to that demand; but even a totalitarian regime cannot work psychological miracles in its citizens.[1]

Stalin could well promise in all sincerity that he would not strive to impose communism on the occupied countries, but the men deputed to give effect to this promise on the spot could not but act in a way which made his words sound like deliberate falsehoods.

---

[1] As early as the beginning of 1946 the author watched this conflict in Eastern Germany and described it in a series of articles. He watched the same conflict, but in reverse, in the British and American Zones, where Military Governors who had been business-men in civilian life gave vent to their revulsion against the at first faintly-socialist flavour of Allied occupation policy.

Thus at least three factors combined to undo Stalin's policy of self-containment: genuine revolutionary ferment abroad; the revolutionary urge in Stalin's own armies; and the jockeying for positions among allies rapidly turning into potential enemies.

The expansion of communism was facilitated by the fact that soon after the war the United States, in part relying on its monopoly in atomic weapons and in part responding to popular pacifism, disbanded its armies and left in Europe only a token occupation force. Stalin now knew that he could go ahead with the establishment of communist regimes, without exposing Russia to effective retaliation from the West. Had he had any ground to fear such retaliation, he would hardly have risked the drift away from self-containment.

So far, the expansion of communism was still confined to the countries which had by common Allied agreement been allotted to the Soviet sphere of influence—Yugoslavia being the only exception. The terms of the Teheran-Yalta-Potsdam pacts had been so ill-defined and vague that Stalin could still maintain that he was acting within his rights and that it was the Western powers who illegitimately tried to interfere in the internal affairs of the Soviet zone. Once again he tried to go back to self-containment, self-containment, that is, within an area expanded in agreement with the Western Allies. He was still confident that beyond that area no revolutionary development would upset or disturb the balance of power which had resulted from the war. He cold-shouldered the embattled Greek communists; and he bluntly urged Tito to withdraw support from them. He believed that he still wielded the magic wand, cracked and split though it was, which would enable him to control the tides of revolution.

Then, in 1948–9, the magic wand finally broke in his hands. The Chinese revolution overtook him; and at a stroke it threw his calculations out of balance and upset the whole international *status quo*.

In February 1948 Stalin confided to Kardelj, Tito's Foreign Minister, that after the war he 'bluntly' told Mao Tse-tung that the Chinese revolution 'had no prospects', that Mao should 'seek a *modus vivendi* with Chiang Kai-shek . . . join the Chiang Kai-shek government, and dissolve the [communist] army'. With an Oriental slyness which matched Stalin's own, Mao listened reverently, nodded approvingly, and, disregarding Stalin's counsel of wisdom and caution, kept his armies in being, raised new ones, and led Chinese communism to its triumph.

Yet Stalin's part in the Chinese revolution was somewhat more complex than his own confidences to Kardelj might suggest.

After Japan's capitulation the Russian armies in Manchuria and Northern China handed over Japanese stores of munitions to Mao's partisans. Without these supplies Mao might not have been able to hold his ground against Chiang Kai-shek, whose troops were equipped and supported by the United States. Thus Stalinist Russia made a direct material contribution to the victory of Chinese communism.

There remains the strange fact that having helped to equip Mao's armies Stalin then urged Mao to disband them. How is this paradox to be accounted for?

Psychologically and morally it was almost impossible for the Soviet troops in Manchuria and Northern China to debar Mao's partisans from the Japanese army stores. The partisans were taking possession of those stores on their own initiative and interference might have led to clashes. Once again Stalin had to surrender to the revolutionary dynamics of the Soviet State and to his own communist reputation.

And once again he was still confident that he was arming merely his pawn, not a force that would make its own revolution. A fairly strong communist army in North China might be a useful instrument of pressure against Chiang Kai-shek and the United States—an expendable bargaining counter. When Stalin thought the moment had come to expend it, he told Mao to lay down arms and to submit to Chiang Kai-shek. But once again the 'pawn' played its own game.

In February 1948, Stalin admitted to Kardelj his 'mistake' over the Chinese revolution. Yet six months later, just before the last phase of the civil war, he repeated the 'mistake' and made a last attempt to hold Mao back.

'As late as July 1948, the Russians neither expected nor desired an immediate communist victory in China. In that month the Chinese Communist Party held a conference to discuss plans for the coming autumn campaign. The advice from Russia was to continue guerrilla warfare for the coming year in order to weaken America, who was expected to continue to pour arms into China in support of the Kuomintang. Russia opposed any plan to end the civil war by taking the large cities. Russian advice was rejected by this conference, the contrary policy was adopted. . . .'[1]

Overtaken by the Chinese revolution, Stalin had to keep after it, to adopt it, father it, and give it all his ideological tenderness. The tenderness had to be all the more effusive because the child knew very well what desperate efforts the 'father' had made to bring about an abortion.

Statesmen in the West at once believed in Stalin's paternity and took at its face value his display of parental virtue. Even after Stalin's death, Mr. John Foster Dulles stated that 'In Asia, Stalin's plans, laid twenty-five years ago, achieved a dramatic success through the communist civil war'. If this were true, Stalin would indeed have

[1] The quotation is from a report in *The Times* (27 June 1950) by a Special Correspondent returned from Peking. This report has been independently checked at another source in fairly close contact with the Chinese communist leaders. The general account of the interplay between domestic Chinese factors and Soviet policy in the Chinese revolution is based on the author's recent study of Chinese communist sources, Maoist and Trotskyist.

deserved to be called the greatest political genius in history. But it is not true.

The appearance that Stalin's *fiat* made and unmade revolutions was kept up by the fact that the victorious Communist Parties rallied to Russia and submitted to the Stalin cult. To Stalin this accretion of power in the middle of his conflict with the West was of course most welcome; and it flattered him to be the Rising Sun over half of Europe and half of Asia, and not just over Russia. The Chinese and Eastern European communists rallied to him because he still represented to them the tradition of the October Revolution that had inspired international communism. An even more decisive motive was their fear of domestic counter-revolutionary forces, or of the counter-revolutionary potentialities of Western policy, or of both. The Communist Parties in power felt that in a divided world they could not stand on their own feet; that they had to lean on Russia, and to accept the Stalin cult. They did so, more often than not, with a trembling heart and fearful forebodings; and they had to sacrifice some of their own leaders to the Moloch of Stalinism.

Tito alone dared to rebel (rather late in the day), because he could rely on strong domestic support, and also because he hoped to find security in a neutral recess between the two blocs. The other communist leaders had neither Tito's self-confidence nor his illusions. Some of them had an acute sense of their own weakness at home; and none appeared to believe that it would be possible for them to survive in a no-man's-land between East and West. Incidentally, the West as well as the East did its utmost to reduce the no-man's-land, with the result that while Stalin inadvertently worked long and hard to produce many Titos, the West did its best to ensure that he should produce but one.

Thus came into being the vast realm of Stalinism

which stretches from the Elbe to the Chinese Sea and is inhabited by nearly 800 million people, five times the number of Russia's population at the beginning of the Stalin era. There was originally no design for this gigantic structure. It piled up while the supposed master builder suffered frequent bouts of absent-mindedness. The edifice grew seemingly of its own accord by a series of historical 'accidents', through which the revolutionary trend of the age performed its work.

Stalin had been willing to content himself with 'socialism in one country'. He had wished to keep Russia in her place and to refrain from antagonizing the world by international revolutionary aspirations. All that he had expected in return was that the world would leave him alone with his Russia. But the tempest of the time drove Russia out of her national shell; and it let loose the furies of revolution which drove Stalin from his retreat, hoisted him to a dizzy eminence, and from there forced him to throw down a challenge to the world.

As the expression of Bolshevism's isolation and self-isolation, Stalinism had been dead and buried long before Stalin died. It fell to Stalin himself to make the long overdue funeral oration on 'socialism in one country', for this is what his last public speech at the Nineteenth Congress of the party in October 1952 amounted to. In it he recalled the far-off days when Soviet Russia had been the only 'Shock Brigade of international communism' and he welcomed and extolled the many new 'Shock Brigades' in Europe and Asia which had since taken their place by Russia's side.

Yet even at this stage he attempted to escape the consequences of a destiny which, he feared, might ruin if not himself then the far-flung realm he was leaving behind.

He tried to revive his old formula of communist self-containment. But this was to be self-containment 'on a higher level', as he himself might have put it—'socialism within one-third of the world' instead of within one country.

He had come to realize that any further expansion of communism would almost certainly lead to a world war, for which Russia was not ready. It is difficult to indicate the last critical point in the development of his policy. It may be that the war in Korea gave him a warning signal of the dangers ahead. But it is by no means certain that the initiative for the attempt to carry communism into southern Korea had come from Stalin—it may have come from Mao. At any rate, in the Korean war Stalin aimed at an international stalemate which would allow his camp to keep its positions without retreating, but also without advancing.

He was anxious that his party, having swallowed so much more than he had intended, should gain the time needed for digestion. He was not the type of conqueror who tries to cure indigestion by swallowing more.

He estimated that two more decades or so were needed to allow Russia to catch up with and surpass the United States industrially, to attain a standard of living that would assure popular contentment, to raise Eastern Europe to an industrial level superior to that of Western Europe, and to allow communist China to develop its economic resources up to the present Russian standard.

He believed that once those goals had been attained, the attraction of communism would become so overwhelming that nothing could stop the whole of Europe and Asia from turning communist. He saw that it was primarily American economic superiority, operating through the Marshall Plan and the Mutual Security agencies, that had defeated communism in Western Europe without much direct political intervention by the United States. On the other hand, Russia, because of her economic inferiority, maintained her preponderance in

Eastern Europe primarily by the direct use of political and even military force. She had had to send out her political police to fight 'dollar diplomacy'.

In what we may suppose to have been Stalin's vision of the years 1965–70 the picture was reversed. He saw a self-sufficient bloc of 800 million people, toiling within the framework of an integrated planned economy, which should in time be able to produce such wealth and attain such high standards of living that communism could rely on its economic preponderance rather than on political or military coercion; while a stagnant or decaying bourgeois West would be losing its power of attraction and would come to rely more and more on the use of force.

Stalin apparently held that to attain this goal it was, on balance, worthwhile for communism to adopt in the meantime a broad policy of self-containment within its third of the globe, especially as the rulers of the other two-thirds were bent on containing it.

These ideas emerge from between the lines of Stalin's last published writings ('The Economic Problems of Socialism in the U.S.S.R.'). In these he came down heavily on the ultra-leftists, the Utopians and the adventurers, as he called them, who were 'dizzy' with Soviet economic power. Against their views, he insisted that the solution of the main economic problems confronting the Soviet Union was a long-term task. Time, time, and once again time was required. The unspoken yet inescapable conclusion of his argument was that in her foreign policy Russia must bargain for a long, a very long breathing space.

It may be assumed that he argued out these ideas in detail and handed them down to his Russian successors, to Mao Tse-tung, and to a few chosen communist leaders of Eastern Europe.

In his last writings one can almost hear the echoes of the debates which Stalin's views provoked among his entourage. 'But will the West give us such a breathing space?' was one obvious objection. Another seems to have run as follows: 'Would it not be more realistic to assume that war in the near future is inevitable? That Russia would not, as in the Second World War, have bourgeois allies to whom she would need to make political concessions? Would she therefore not be better advised, in the interest of self-preservation, to press on with world revolution and to encourage further communist expansion?'

To such arguments and objections Stalin replied with an explicit and emphatic 'No'. He argued publicly and at great length that the capitalist countries would cut each other's throats rather than attack Russia. War between the capitalist countries was still 'inevitable', he said; but their joint crusade against the communist bloc was not. In itself the argument was incongruous and scholastic, as Stalin's argumentation usually was. But in this particular context it had a definite meaning and it pursued a practical aim. It was an argument in favour of buying breathing space from the West, in favour of communist self-containment.

Thus Stalin's last writings might be described as his political testament. He said in effect to his heirs: Your estate is one-third of the world. Keep it, preserve it, and build it up into a power which will eventually daunt all your enemies. In the meantime beware of hotheads and adventurers. Do not take risks. Do not rush into revolutionary enterprises in which you may dissipate what you possess.

In this shrewd caution Stalin remained true to himself to the end. During his life-time history sometimes proved him right; but more than once it mocked his caution and made of him the strangest of adventurers. Is history perhaps for the last time going to mock his caution posthumously? Will Stalin's successors be willing or able to carry out his political testament?

PART TWO

RUSSIA IN TRANSITION

CHAPTER SIX

THE MORAL CLIMATE

THE crisis which Stalin's death accelerated and brought into the open was caused by a fundamental change in the relation between rulers and ruled. Before the Stalin era Bolshevism, in its aspirations and outlook, towered above its native Russian environment. Then it levelled itself with that environment and transformed it, with the paradoxical result that towards the end of the Stalin era the nation was culturally superior to the method of government and the moral climate of Stalinism. At first Bolshevism debased itself into Stalinism in order to be in harmony with Russia. Then Russia had to suffer permanent self-abasement to keep in line with Stalinism.

The fact that the nation had outgrown Stalinist tutelage was at the root of the acute malaise of the last years and months of the Stalin era. This malaise, which even the outsider could sense, did not express itself in clear political terms. There was no articulate opposition to the Stalinist system of government. After decades of terror all potential centres of opposition had been destroyed. No group existed capable of formulating any independent political programme and acting on it. Society as a whole had lost the capacity and the habit of forming its own opinion. As society's guardian Stalin exercised control so tyrannically that he deprived his ward of any intrinsic political identity. In time Soviet society grew tired of the harness of Stalinism and was anxious to throw it off; but it had also grown so accustomed to the harness that it could take no step without it. This ambivalent attitude towards Stalinism characterizes the period of transition to a new era.

We cannot say how long the period of transition may last. It may take Russia a few years to overcome her political numbness and to grow articulate again. If one were to judge Russia's state of mind by the cacophony of meaningless slogans put out by various groups of Soviet refugees to the West, the outlook would be unpromising indeed. But such a judgment would be absurd. Hardly any of those refugees belonged to the political or intellectual élite of their nation and in this respect they can in no way be compared to the émigrés of the pre-revolutionary era. Sooner or later, the Russian people will learn to form and express its own opinions; and once it begins to do so, it will progress at a breathtaking pace and astonish the world once again by the extraordinary fertility of its political mind.

In the meantime, however, the initiative lies entirely with the men of the ruling group. Only reform decreed from above can force a way out of the impasse into which Stalinism finally landed itself. Moreover, reform from above forestalls upheaval from below. The first moves of Malenkov's government have shown an awareness of this fact.

The Stalinist method of government cannot be continued now. Some of its features had been accepted in apathy by a primitive, uneducated people; but they cannot be imposed on a people about to come of age politically and culturally. Other features may have been justified once by the needs of Russia's economic and social development; but now they have become impediments to further progress.

Stalinism has exhausted its historical function. Like every other great revolution, the Russian revolution has made ruthless use of force and violence to bring into being a new social order and to ensure its survival. An old-established regime relies for its continuance on the force of social custom. A revolutionary order creates new custom by force. Only when its material framework has been firmly set and consolidated can it rely on its own inherent vitality; then it frees itself from the terror that formerly safeguarded it.

When the force of economic circumstances guarantees the survival of the new order, the use of physical force tends to become an anachronism. The cruel dictatorship which has abolished with blood and iron any possibility of a return to pre-revolutionary conditions must then end. If it struggles to perpetuate itself, its defeat is certain. This was the course of the English revolution in the seventeenth and of the French in the eighteenth century; and this has also been the course of the Russian revolution. The deeper the social upheaval it has brought about and the wider its scope, the longer is the period during which a revolution clings to terror. This period has lasted tragically long in Russia, much longer than it did in France.

We have analysed in detail one aspect of this development. We have seen how Stalinism abolished the rural smallholding and set up the collective farm by sheer force. For many years the new structure was very shaky and might have collapsed had it not been buttressed by violence and held together by iron bands. But while Stalinism was waging an implacable war against all opponents of collectivization it also produced the new economic conditions, the machinery, the agronomic services, and the economic habits, which were sure eventually to enable collective farming to carry on under its own steam. Now, even extreme opponents of collectivization begin to realize that for Russia there is no way back to the privately owned smallholding, except at the price of national suicide.

The same is more or less true of the whole structure of Soviet society, in particular of its enormous publicly owned and planned economy. One need not accept the

Stalinist myth that socialism has been established in Russia. Still less need one take at its face value the ludicrous claim that the Soviet Union is in 'transition from socialism to communism'. But it is true that the framework for a socialist society, which was altogether lacking in the Leninist era, now exists; and it has been consolidated.

Precisely because of this, the methods used to bring about the present state of affairs have now become both useless and harmful; and the awareness that this is so must have grown and spread among the Soviet people.

One of the most difficult and explosive issues of the Stalin era was the great economic inequality prevalent in Soviet society; and this is likely to remain the most difficult problem in the post-Stalin period also.

The message of the October Revolution was implicitly egalitarian. Whatever the Stalinist arguments or even the original Marxist texts may say against 'levelling', the Russian workers and peasants backed the revolution and rallied to its defence because they took it for granted that the new regime would satisfy their longing for equality. This has been the attitude of the proletarian or plebeian masses in every revolution.

The Bolshevik regime could not help but frustrate the instinctive egalitarianism of the masses. There were not enough of the material necessities of life to go round. To take only one example: before the Five Year Plans were initiated the Russian footwear industry did not manufacture more than about 30 million pairs of shoes and boots per year. Small artisans produced perhaps another 30 million pairs. This was just sufficient to supply one pair to every third Soviet citizen. The other two had to go barefoot, or to make their own bast shoes as the *muzhiks* usually did. This is a typical example because the same or a similar relation between social need and effective supply prevailed in many other essential consumer industries.

'A pair of boots for only one out of every three citizens'' this was the formula which expressed the inevitability of Stalinist anti-egalitarianism. The barefooted and the owner of a pair of shoes are not equal; and not even a government consisting of communist angels could make them so. The government had to set out to build the factories which would produce enough footwear, clothing, dwellings, etc., for all. If the machines, the buildings, the raw materials, the power stations, and the labour force needed were not available, as they were not in Russia, the government had to start building the factories that would one day produce the machines and the power plants. It had to develop the sources of raw materials and to train industrial labour. In the meantime it had to distribute the available footwear, either directly, or indirectly, by means of a differential wage scale, among the people whose services were essential to the State and the economy. Moreover, it had to defend the man with the shoes against the natural jealousy and hostility of the barefooted.

It was in the national interest that the government should foster a privileged minority consisting of administrators, planners, engineers, and skilled workers. The development of the country's resources depended on them; and they would not have worked without incentive.

Inequality, once encouraged, takes care of itself; the privileged minority seeks to enlarge its privileges. The Soviet bureaucrat, technician, or skilled worker was not satisfied with one pair of shoes—he wanted to have two or three. The same applied to clothing, housing, medical facilities, and so on.

As long as the government was bent on expanding coal-mines and steel mills, producer industries and armament plants, the building up of consumer industries was deferred. Inequality grew and assumed shocking proportions. The greater the scarcity of goods and the more primitive the level of civilization, the more brutal was the scramble for privileges. We know that Russia's urban population grew by about 45 million during the Stalin era. Relatively few houses were built; and during the war many cities and towns were razed by the enemy. The overwhelming majority of the people therefore was, and still is, condemned to live in the most appalling conditions. The few tolerable, good, or luxurious dwellings were allotted to skilled workers, technicians, and bureaucrats.

A more humane government than Stalin's might have tried to promote consumer industries even at the cost of a somewhat slower rate of expansion in basic materials and producer goods. But when the history of these decades, with their armaments fever and war-time destruction, is viewed in retrospect, it seems doubtful that any government would have been able to improve the situation radically, unless it abandoned industrialization altogether or slowed it down to the point of endangering national interest; and this would have resulted in an even lower standard of living for the vast majority than the present.

Stalinism took upon itself the daring and dramatic task of imposing inequality on a people which had just carried out the greatest of all revolutions in the name of equality. This imposition was naturally received with indignation. The old Bolsheviks who had been accustomed to identify themselves with the egalitarian aspirations of the masses branded it as a betrayal of the revolution. Since they spoke with the authority of great revolutionaries their criticism was doubly dangerous to Stalin's policy. Reacting against the clamour for equality Stalinism established a cult of inequality. It was not satisfied with pointing out that egalitarianism would lead to economic stagnation. It declared categorically that the privileges of the minority were of the essence of socialism and it branded the defenders of egalitarianism as agents of counter-revolution. In this way Stalinism freed its hands to provide material incentives in plenty and in excess to administrators, managers, technicians, and skilled workers.

With the passing of time, however, inequality, carried to extreme, tended to change from a progressive into a reactionary factor. It began to hamper Russia's economic development instead of furthering it. It kept the vast majority in a state of apathy and sullenness. Moreover, it rapidly lost its initial justification. The relation between social need and effective supply is now no longer a pair of shoes for only one out of every three Soviet citizens. (The output of the footwear industry has in recent years been sufficient to supply every citizen with at least one pair per year.) Enough essential consumer goods are now being produced to satisfy a very wide range of needs; and far more can be produced in the immediate future.

It is a point of only academic interest whether or when equality may become materially possible. Incentive wages and salaries will remain indispensable for a long time to come. But there is certainly room for eliminating the glaring inequalities of the Stalin era.

In the initial phases of 'socialist accumulation' it was possible for the government to tell the people that they must tighten their belts and even starve while they were building the new factories. Stalin's successors cannot continue to demand such heavy sacrifices. The factories are there already; the capacity to produce is there; and the will to produce is also there. Most of Russia's basic and heavy industries are at a level comparable to that of American industry fifteen or twenty years ago; but her consumer industries are far below it. This disproportion is bound to produce a national crisis, unless it is reduced in the next few years.

The protracted Stalinist campaign against the egalitarian heresy has tended to defeat itself. A great cry for equality is about to go up. Audible in whispers even in the last two or three years, it interjected itself into the discussions on the 'transition from socialism to communism', to which there was much more than mere propaganda or dogmatic hair-splitting. The new Soviet generation has been taught to regard its present way of life as socialism and it has been led to believe that inequality will be eliminated under communism, the next phase of development. During recent years, discussion in academic institutions, workers' clubs, and party cells has centred on the seemingly unreal question: How rapidly can the transition from socialism to communism be effected? This was only another way, indeed the only permissible way, of asking when and how the present inequalities would be reduced and eliminated.

Stalin's Politbureau at first put out this slogan about transition to communism in a spirit of self-congratulation and self-advertisement. 'Look how far forward we have brought you!' it said to the people. At most it wished to provide the intelligentsia and the workers with a theme for harmless dogmatic debate. But once the debate began it was anything but 'harmless'. The theme attracted and absorbed the unspoken hopes and suppressed egalitarian yearnings. The intelligentsia and the workers had been officially encouraged to indulge in a vision of the future; and they projected into that vision all their grievances against the present. They began to voice the old egalitarian heresy and other 'unorthodox ideas' for the professing of which, whether real or suspected, innumerable men and women had paid with their lives in the late 1930's.

Analysing a great debate on communism which took place at the Economics Institute of Moscow's Academy of Science, the present author wrote in the summer of 1951:[1]

'Visions of the future have a capricious logic of their own. This is true even in a country whose most eminent liberal historian, Miliukov, once said that its social classes

[1] From a series of articles on mid-century Russia published in *The Reporter* (New York), August-November 1951.

and even its thoughts and ideas had always been the product of official decrees or official inspiration. A government may find it easy and expedient to encourage its subjects to indulge in a certain sort of dream as an escape from ugly realities. It may even prescribe, as the Kremlin now does, what the subject ought to dream. But it finds it much harder to intervene in the actual course of the dream and to make it wholly conform to order. Its subjects may begin to see images long banished and to murmur the most terrible heresies in their sleep. . . . As speaker after speaker tried to produce an answer [to the question about the transition to communism], the ghosts of banished heresies crowded into the conference hall . . . at that seat of Stalinist learning, the Economics Institute.' Incidentally, this debate and the heresies voiced in it came under severe attack in the last months of Stalin's life.

Alongside the collectivization of farming and the forcible training of peasants as industrial workers, the need to enforce inequality invested the Stalinist terror with its prodigious momentum and pervasiveness. The terror matched the resistance which those policies encountered. Only with scorpions could tens of millions be driven into collective farms, multitudes be shifted to new industrial sites, and the vast majority of the people be forced to toil in misery and to suppress in silence the fury evoked by the privileges of a minority. The terror worked ruthlessly, sometimes blindly, but on the whole effectively. It owed its effectiveness to a moral backing as well as to the sheer mechanical weight of repression. The government had identified itself with a great national cause, or, as the Marxist would put it, with an historical necessity. This identification, in the last instance, accounted for the helplessness of the Soviet people against the terror, and for the complicity of the politically decisive elements, the party and the army.

But proportionately to the degree in which the government succeeded in enforcing inequality the necessity for the terror employed to enforce it decreased. The growing awareness of this process, even in the ruling group, has in recent years been reflected in the arguments over the tempo at which the State may 'wither away' in the transition to communism. Behind this dogmatic formula loomed the practical and insistent question: When are we going to mitigate the rigours of our criminal codes? When are we going to soften the draconic discipline in our factories, collective farms, offices, and schools? When are we going to sweep away our concentration camps?

Another source of the strength of Stalinism—Soviet Russia's isolation—has also run dry. The emergence of new communist regimes beyond Russia's frontiers has had profound repercussions inside Russia. Stalinism had justified its despotism with the argument that, as the sole bulwark of proletarian revolution, Russia was surrounded by a hostile world. The argument had great power: it disarmed or paralysed innumerable recalcitrant minds. It was, after all, true that twice within living memory German armies had marched towards the Dnieper and the Volga. It was also true that in its first days the revolution had had to struggle for existence against French, British, and even American intervention, against a blockade, a commercial and financial boycott, and a *cordon sanitaire*. Stalinism throve on the popular memory of these unhappy events. It kept alive that memory and fanned the smouldering hatreds and fears that went with it.

However, when new communist regimes had formed vast 'security belts' around Russia, in Asia and Eastern and Central Europe, it was no longer so easy to invoke isolation and capitalist encirclement as the justification for the harshness of Stalinism. For the first time in decades Russia seemed secure from foreign threats. For a short spell fear of American monopoly in atomic

weapons once again appeared to justify in the eyes of the
Russian people the Stalinist attitude towards the world.
But this fear, too, soon subsided.

Even a regime armed with all the machinery of totalitarian control needs its moral justification. Without this,
popular disillusionment and resentment clog and slow
down the totalitarian machine. Fear of American atomic
supremacy helped to keep the wheels of the machine
turning, but they were not turning with their old
impetus.

Yet such is the power of inertia that institutions and
methods of government outlast the causes that have
brought them into being; and they struggle to outlast
them. In its last years and months Stalinism fought desperately to keep its hold on Russia. In doing so, it
parodied its own previous performances, revealed its own
grotesqueness, and betrayed its weakness. Before its
extinction Stalinism experienced a spasm of deceptive
vigour which contorted its face into a last repulsive
grimace.

In these final years the primitive magic of Stalinism
made an insolent mockery of Russia. The cult of the
Leader assumed so nauseating and nightmarish a quality,
especially after the celebration of Stalin's seventieth
birthday in 1949, that it is difficult to describe it. For
nearly two years the columns of *Pravda*, for instance,
were filled with birthday greetings to the septuagenarian
deity. No Soviet author, journalist, scientist or general
dared to write even a few sentences without referring to
the Father of the Peoples, the Greatest and the Wisest
Genius. An outsider could not help wondering how the
Soviet people could put up with these wild extrava-
gances of adulation, especially when the same issues of
Pravda reported that 57 million Soviet citizens were
receiving education in schools of all grades. How—one
reflected—could the primitive magic of Stalinism 'co-
exist' with modern knowledge and Marxist theories in
the minds of millions?

The same air of bizarre unreality hung over the orgy of nationalism of these last years. The Russian people were constantly and insistently told that they, and they alone, were the salt of the earth; that they, and only they, had made all the great scientific and technological discoveries and initiated all the great philosophical, sociological, and other ideas. If such propaganda had been addressed to an illiterate people one might believe that it could be effective in some measure. But it could not possibly find much credence in a Russia in which the revolution and then Stalinism itself had aroused an insatiable thirst for knowledge. Nationalist self-glorification might have suited the isolated and self-centred Soviet people of the early years of the Stalin era, when, as a rule, it was not indulged in. But such self-glorification was quite out of date in 1950–2, when Russia's destiny had become inextricably bound up with that of the rest of the world. Even from the Stalinist viewpoint, it could not be reconciled with the spreading of revolution abroad. One-third of mankind already lived under communist regimes, and Stalinism spoke as if its realm had been confined to the old Tambov *gubernia* or to the Tula district. All account of time seemed to have been lost in the Kremlin.

Equally parochial and anachronistic was the interference of Stalinist dogma with biology, chemistry, physics, linguistics, philosophy, economics, literature, and the arts. This interference, more obtrusive and noisier than at any earlier stage, was reminiscent of the days when the Inquisition decided for the whole Christian world which were the right and the wrong ideas about God, the universe, and man. The intrusion of theological or bureaucratic dogma on the working of the scientific mind belongs essentially to a pre-industrial epoch. In contemporary Russia it amounted to virtual sabotage of science and technology. It was possible only because the rulers who had taken charge of Russia's education were themselves inadequately educated; and

Stalin behaved like a half-educated, capricious guardian constantly tampering with the curriculum of his ward and imposing his own fancies and tastes.

But even while Stalin was alive it was easy to see that the primitive magic of Stalinism was losing its last battle. The heresy hunt was never at a standstill and yet it was producing little effect. Its victims did not suffer the cruel fate of their unhappy predecessors of the 1930's. There were no new purge trials in Russia, although such trials were staged in Budapest, Prague, and Sofia. As a rule the 'deviationists' were not imprisoned or deported. They were required to confess the error of their ways and were punished by some mild form of demotion. Sometimes the government honoured them with the highest awards only a short time after they had been singled out for attack. Even the confessions of error were different in kind from those to which Russia had become accustomed earlier on. Having uttered the conventional words of recantation, the 'deviationists' often defended themselves and their views in a veiled yet transparent manner. This seems to have been the regular pattern from the time of the attack on Professor Varga, the well-known economist, in 1946, up to the campaigns against the unorthodox biologists, linguists, musicians, and others. A notable exception was the case of Voznessensky, the disgraced member of the Politbureau and chief economic planner, who completely disappeared from the public eye.

Those who viewed the Russia of Stalin's last years through the prism of the 1930's saw in the heresy hunts a repetition of the great purges and hardly noticed their very different and much milder consequences.

What was the reason for this relative mildness?

In the first instance, the new heresies contained no immediate or visible threat to the regime, let alone to Stalin's position. In this they differed from the genuinely political 'deviations' of earlier periods inspired by Stalin's real rivals and opponents. Since the suppression

of the latter, Stalin's position was so secure that he could
well afford to show a certain degree of indulgence.

On the other hand, the new opposition to Stalinist
orthodoxy, predominantly intellectual, was so widespread
and elusive that it could not be uprooted without a blood
bath similar to that of the 1930's, if not worse. This
would have entailed disastrous consequences to the
State, the economy, and morale. As Stalin could not risk
such consequences, the new heresy hunt amounted to
little more than shadow-boxing. It was just enough to
irritate the intelligentsia; to keep it in a state of suspense;
to feed and fan its resentments; and to speed up its
spiritual alienation from Stalinism.

About a hundred years ago Alexander Herzen, the
great Russian revolutionary, wrote that the West saw
only Russia's government and façade but had no inkling
of her people. He blamed the secretiveness of the Russian government for this but also the West's superficiality
and partisanship. Herzen's observation has not lost its
topicality. Behind the façade of rigid official uniformity,
the attitude of the Russian people towards Stalinism has
been so complex as to elude the over-simplified formulæ
of Western propagandists during the cold war.

The people 'behind the façade' were and are proud of
the achievements of the Stalin era, and deeply attached
to what was and has remained great and universal in the
Russian revolution; and at the same time they suffocated
in the stuffy air of Stalinist despotism.

The craving for a purifying change in the moral
climate grew not only among the ruled: it infected many
of the rulers as well. The bureaucracy felt oppressed
by the anachronistic methods of Stalinism as much as
the workers and the peasants did, or even more. The
educated, intelligent men in the civil service had been
deprived of all initiative and the right to exercise their
own judgment and talent. They had to couch their ideas
and aspirations carefully in arid and turgid official lingo.
They had to speak with Stalin's voice instead of with

their own. They were constantly harassed by a mania for secrecy which reached its greatest intensity during the last years: it became a 'State crime' for any official to divulge the most trivial fact about national life or governmental work. (Secrecy is usually the weapon of the weak, anxious to conceal weakness from a stronger enemy. Like so many other devices of Stalinism, it had its relative justification when Russia was really weak; but it has been rapidly losing any such justification with the growth of Russian power.)

Soviet publications reflected these strains and stresses only negatively and indirectly, and still do so even after Stalin's death. Thus, for instance, the March 1953 issue of the *Kommunist* (the former *Bolshevik*) says:

'We must definitely put an end to opportunistic indifference and eliminate the anti-Marxist theory that the class struggle is calming down, a theory which starts from the premiss that as we are moving forward towards communism, even though we are doing so in capitalistic encirclement, the enemy becomes more and more harmless. . . .'

The polemical distortion of the criticized view is obvious enough; but one would look in vain for any exposition in the Soviet Press of this view or for any indication of the persons holding it. Another paper, brought out some time before Stalin's death, castigated members of the intelligentsia—their names and academic titles were given—who set out unorthodox views in special memoranda and circulated these in typescript among friends and even in official institutions. This detail revealed more about the actual ferment of ideas than reams of Stalinist and anti-Stalinist writings. It indicated a relaxation of totalitarian control: no one would have dared thus to circulate unorthodox views under his own signature in the late 1930's or perhaps even in the 1940's.

Such attempts to propagate heretical ideas are in line with a good old Russian tradition. A hundred years ago

Russia's progressive thinkers, unable to air their views in the licensed Press, similarly circulated their manuscripts, which made history. It was in this way that, for instance, Belinsky, the great radical critic and precursor of revolutionary trends, spread his ideas under the rule of Nicholas I, the Iron Tsar.

Unlike their predecessors, however, the Belinskys of contemporary Russia, if they exist, can be only reformers, not revolutionaries. They can aim only at improving and cleansing the existing social order, not at overthrowing it. That the main trend of Soviet anti-Stalinism was reformist could be seen even in the distorting mirror of recent émigré writings. Some time ago the Russian émigré Press reported that by far the most numerous party among post-war Russian refugees was one which described itself as the 'Lenin Party' and advocated a return to the democratic origins of the Bolshevik revolution. Hostile correspondents who reported this pointed out with some alarm that 'at least a good half' of the mass of refugees belonged to that party, although it had no periodicals and no organization, and although its adherents in the camps for displaced persons lived in constant terror of being denounced either to Soviet or to Western 'security organs'.

The 'Lenin legend' is surviving the Stalin cult, although the latter cynically exploited and abused it for its own purposes. It is difficult to define the implications of this fact. Leninism is subject to widely differing interpretations; and it may be held that the slogan about a 'return to Lenin' is unreal: history rarely, if ever, returns to its starting-point. But what the slogan sums up is a yearning for regeneration of 'Soviet democracy' and a desire to reform the present order, not to overthrow it.

The strength of the 'Lenin legend' may be judged from many indications. We can cite here one other instance which seems as convincing as it is strange. It will be remembered that during the Second World War the

Soviet General A. Vlasov, taken prisoner by the Nazis, later fought on the German side and commanded a Russian army formed of prisoners of war. After the war Vlasov was handed over to Soviet military authorities and executed as a traitor. Recently a book on Vlasov was published by a Russian émigré who was Vlasov's adjutant and was by his side when the Nazis conducted him from a prison camp to Berlin. The author describes that on the way Vlasov argued thus with the German officers who were escorting him: 'I want to give you my advice on how to overthrow Stalin. This can be done only with the help of Lenin.' There was, Vlasov said, only one way of gaining the confidence of the Soviet people, and this was to tell them that Stalin had distorted and falsified Lenin's teaching, and that the time had come to restore the true Leninist republic of workers and peasants. 'We ought to tell the people that we are going to begin anew where the great Lenin left off—if Lenin had been alive everything would have been different.'

It is difficult to imagine a scene of greater bathos than this, in which a Soviet general, setting his foot on the slippery road of treason, pleaded with the Nazis that *they* should appeal to the Russian people in the name of Lenin. Vlasov hated the Stalin regime and allowed himself to be carried away by this hatred. The Nazis were willing to use him, but, of course, his advice sounded to them like the raving of a disordered mind. No anti-communist power could risk conjuring up the spirit of Lenin. Nevertheless there was a great truth behind Vlasov's grotesque pleading: The hope of a renascence of the revolution has never been extinguished in the Soviet people, and it has been kept alive by remote memories of the Leninist period. This hope still remains an imponderable and most vital factor in the political climate of Russia.

Significantly during Stalin's last months there resounded throughout Russia a warning against those who argued that now, when Russia was no longer the only communist country in the world, the old ways and habits of Stalinism had become outdated. With one foot in the grave, Stalin heard his lieutenants raising the alarm about the recurrence of 'Bukharinist and Trotskyist deviations' in the party. And Stalin himself, in his last published letters, had to rebuke young Soviet economists for a relapse into these long-suppressed heresies.

At that late stage, barely two months before Stalin's death, the story about the 'plot' of the Kremlin doctors burst upon Russia. Its specific political meaning will be discussed later—here we are concerned only with its bearing upon the moral crisis of Stalinism.

It is not certain whether or to what extent Stalin himself was responsible for the frame-up. But, regardless of this, in the eyes of Russia and of the world Stalinism reduced itself to a ghastly absurdity through this incident. It committed moral suicide even before the physical death of its author. The official revelations about the 'plot' looked like an attempt to re-enact in Moscow the Witches' Sabbath of the 1930's. As has been pointed out before, the purge trials of the 1930's could not be repeated in the Russia of the early 1950's without ruining the regime, the economy, and the morale of the country. A repetition would have clashed so obviously with Russia's interests and frame of mind that a reaction against it, unthinkable earlier, had to come.

The untamed nationalism of recent years was also driven to a self-destructive extreme during the campaign about the doctors' plot. The tale about the anti-Soviet conspiracy of world Jewry had the flavour of the Protocols of the Elders of Zion and of the concoctions of Goebbels's Ministry of Propaganda. It provided grist to the mills of those anti-communists who had always maintained that there was no difference between Stalinism and Nazism and now argued that the inherent kinship of the two was 'bound' to make Stalinism adopt the tenets of racial hatred and anti-Semitism. The argument was superficial and fallacious: it ignored the socialist background of Soviet Russia and the contradictions in the educational influence of Stalinism.

A government which ordered the printing of the works of Marx, Engels, and Lenin in millions of copies, which included these works in the obligatory educational *curriculum* and forced them into the hands of adult citizens, could not walk the road to which 'the doctors' plot' pointed. It could afford to make tactical twists and turns, including the bargain with Hitler in 1939, as long as it could excuse its actions by reference to the needs of national defence. It could exploit episodically and allusively even anti-Semitic prejudice, as it did during the great purges. But it could not strike openly at the very roots of its own ideology. It could debase Marxian internationalism; it could combine it ambiguously with nationalist self-adulation; but it could not attack it directly and frontally.

Before embracing racialism and anti-Semitism any Soviet government would first have to ban the works of Marx, Engels, and Lenin, that is to say to destroy its own birth certificate and ideological title deeds. As Stalinism had not done this, its last scandal served only to underline its own decomposition and to prepare a revulsion against it.

CHAPTER SEVEN

MALENKOV AND HIS ROLE

MALENKOV'S government took the initiative of reform already in the first weeks of its existence. In doing so it may have acted under popular pressure; but the pressure was not apparent. It was not the 'voice of the people' that made Stalin's successors act as they did, for that voice could not be heard. Malenkov's government seemed rather to have guessed the hopes and expectations that were in the people's mind. If any voices did in fact demand reform, they came from the bureaucracy itself or rather from its uppermost stratum.

As representative of that stratum Malenkov came to the fore and to all intents and purposes assumed the succession.

Who is Georgi Maximilianovich Malenkov?

His previous career strongly suggested that he was merely Stalin's shadow, with no political personality of his own.

Almost nothing significant is known about his background, upbringing, and early days. His origins are wrapped in the same obscurity in which Stalin's once were. Like Stalin, he hails from a border zone between Europe and Asia, from the Urals. There may be a hint of non-Russian descent in his patronymic: Maximilian is hardly the name of a 'pure' Russian. In his late teens Malenkov joined the Red Army and the party, and he was a junior political commissar during the civil war in Turkestan. In the early and middle 1920's he studied at the Moscow Institute of Technology.

The Institute, like all other academic establishments in the capital, was astir with inner party controversy. Trotsky had appealed to young communists, especially to students, against the triumvirate of Stalin, Zinoviev, and Kamenev, and warned the young party men about the danger of a 'political degeneration' of the ruling group. The appeal did not fail to evoke response. Trotsky had ardent followers among the communist students. The anti-Trotskyists listened to Bukharin rather than to Stalin, whose theoretical argumentation was uninspiring and pedestrian. It seems that Malenkov, like Zhdanov, his supposed rival in later years, was one of the very few students who took their cue direct from Stalin's General Secretariat.

In his more mature years Malenkov became a member of that Secretariat, the hub of the organization through which Stalin ruled the country. There Malenkov studied the technology of monolithic government. In the course of many years he carefully assimilated Stalin's manner of dealing with men and situations, his administrative methods, and even his mannerisms. Like his master, he shunned great theoretical conceptions of policy and public debates about them. He learned the art of empirical policy-making in a narrow, closely knit group of leaders who viewed ideas primarily from the angle of administrative necessity or convenience.

The ideas often clashed with professed principles and with what the party propagandists were saying. Stalin's policy always had two aspects: one was esoteric, occult; the other was exoteric, designed for mass consumption. His secretaries had to master both aspects, and never confuse them in their own minds. The exoteric aspect might appear baffling, incoherent, even downright stupid. But the *illuminati* knew what Stalin was aiming at at any particular moment; and the most initiated operated the enormous machinery of the party from the General Secretariat.

In the late 1930's Malenkov was already in charge of

the party 'cadres'. It was his responsibility to assign 'the
right man to the right job' at every turn of policy. On
Stalin's behalf, he already held the party in his hands and
wielded much greater influence than did the members of
the Politbureau who on ceremonial occasions appeared
at the Lenin Mausoleum by Stalin's side. As early as
1939 Malenkov brought about the dismissal of Mrs.
Molotov from a Ministerial post—he had attacked her
publicly for mismanaging her department. His position
was becoming similar to that which Stalin had held under
Lenin. But to keep his influence and to enlarge it,
Malenkov had to behave towards Stalin with the utmost
discretion and modesty and to show no sign of
vacillation, let alone of independence. Only as Stalin's
shadow could he continue to gather power in his own
hands.

He had taken over the management of the 'cadres' at
the time of the great purges, when most of the old party
personnel was destroyed or demoted and vacancies had
to be filled with new men. The key-men in the party
machine of the late 1930's and 1940's were therefore
'Malenkov men'. In this respect Malenkov's position was
already stronger than Stalin's in the early and middle
1920's, because at that time Stalin had still to eliminate
his opponents from the party machine and to fill the
decisive posts with his minions.

Stalin deliberately fashioned Malenkov's career so
that it should appear as similar to his own as possible. He
seemed bent on forming Malenkov in his own image, and
he projected, as it were, certain landmarks of his own
life into the life of Malenkov. He gave Malenkov the
same assignments with which he himself had been en-
trusted by Lenin. During the Second World War he
sent Malenkov to the same critical front-line areas that
he himself had inspected in the civil war, including
Stalingrad, his old Tsaritsyn. The Tsaritsyn episode of
1918 had been vested by Stalin's hagiographers with so
much symbolic significance and with so great a halo that,

in the eyes of people brought up in the Stalin cult, Malenkov's mission to Stalingrad at once transferred to him the glories of the young Stalin. In truth, Malenkov's merits as the political commissar responsible for the battle of Stalingrad were more serious and real than the merits which Stalin claimed for himself in connection with the defence of Tsaritsyn in 1918.

Little can be said about the supposed rivalry between Malenkov and Zhdanov in later years. Unlike Malenkov, Zhdanov had the ambitions of the intellectual and the theoretician; and this difference in their outlook may have led to a rivalry faintly, but only very faintly, reminiscent of that between Stalin and Trotsky. Being in charge of the party organization in Leningrad, Zhdanov was somewhat removed from the levers of power at the centre, and his chances against Malenkov were hardly serious. After Zhdanov's death, Malenkov's ascendancy was secure, but he still had to contend against the old Stalin guard headed by Molotov, who could claim seniority in the party hierarchy. Stalin himself had apparently overridden this claim when, at the Nineteenth Congress of the party, in October 1952, he conspicuously threw his mantle over Malenkov's shoulders and let Malenkov make on behalf of the Central Committee the report which used to be made by Lenin and afterwards by Stalin.

But was Malenkov nothing more than Stalin's political projection?

He has certainly been the product of Stalinism and of Stalinism alone. But in his personality the diverse elements of Stalinism, progressive and retrogressive, seem to be in conflict. It is possible that in his mind the vital demands of the new Soviet society and State revolted against the primitive magic and the bureaucratic rigidity of Stalinism. Not only the people but even the bureaucracy, or perhaps especially the bureaucracy, felt acutely the need for rationalization in all spheres of national life, in the working of the administration, in the running of the economy, in the relation between the rulers and the ruled, and in the conduct of foreign policy.

Malenkov's first moves, made since his assumption of power, seem to have gone halfway to meet that need. He has come to the fore in the role of the rationalizer striving to put in order the Stalinist legacy and to disentangle its great assets from its heavy liabilities.

The prerequisite for this is a break with the ecclesiastical outlook of Stalinism, with those scholastic-bureaucratic habits of thought and action which had ensnared the party and clogged the whole machinery of government. It may be a sign of the time that Stalin's successor is one who has received his education at a Technological Institute, not at a Theological Seminary. During the industrial revolution Malenkov was certainly more in his element than his master could have been. His task in 1941–2 was to organize the disrupted Soviet industry for the mass production of tanks. Stalin's assignment at a comparable critical juncture, in 1918, was to requisition grain from the peasants of the Kuban and to transport it to starving Moscow. Each of these assignments was of the utmost importance in its time. But the difference between them reflects the distance which separated two epochs and two generations. In 1918 the survival of the Soviet regime depended on the most primitive economic devices; in 1942 it could be secured only by the work of an enormous and up-to-date industrial organization. If the style of the man offers any clue to his character, then Malenkov's manner is free from the incongruities and the canonical undertones characteristic of Stalin. It is more business-like, clear, and modern, although at times it seems even flatter than Stalin's style.

Stalin was a slave to his own past, to his old heresy hunts and blood feuds. He could do nothing to disavow any part of his record. He approached every new task with an eye on his past performances. In the 1930's he had to justify the Stalin of the 1920's; and in the 1940's and 1950's he still had to justify the Stalin of the 1930's.

He carried the terrible burden of responsibility for the great purges; and he made the whole of Russia share the burden with him. He could do nothing that might throw on those purges retrospectively a light different from that in which he wanted Russia to see them; and any breath of freedom threatened to make Russia see them in a different light.

In the meantime there has grown up a new generation whom Stalin's blood feuds leave indifferent, even if it accepts the Stalinist version of them. The men and women who have entered public life in the last fifteen years know that before their entry a devastating storm had raged in party and State; but they know next to nothing about the issues that were at stake. The independent-minded among them desire nothing more than to think out new problems on their merits, paying no regard to the requirements of an orthodoxy based on past controversies and struggles. Most often they do not even comprehend those requirements, and because of this they have sometimes unwittingly come into conflict with the Stalinist orthodoxy.

In his early fifties, Malenkov stands halfway between the Old Stalin Guard and this new generation. The past has a claim on him, but the claim is not so heavy as to make him unresponsive to the needs of the present. He was implicated in every phase of Stalinism: in the struggle against the oppositions, in the process of collectivization, in the great purges, and in the recent heresy hunts. But in the worst phases he was involved only as a subordinate, not as an initiator; and so he may, up to a point, disclaim responsibility for them. On the other hand, he has owed too much to Stalinism and has himself been too much its product to be able to break away from it openly. He can only sneak away from Stalinism.

His behaviour raises the question: What was his genuine attitude towards Stalinism while Stalin was alive? Was he the zealous and devoted coadjutor he acted? Or did he act his part with carefully concealed mental reservations?

Both assumptions may be true, but each would apply to a different time. Among Stalin's closest supporters and friends there were some who had at first given him their full backing because his policies—socialism in one country, industrialization, and collectivization—had genuinely appealed to them; and Stalin had seemed the right man to give effect to those policies. They had not expected him to become the destroyer of the Old Leninist Guard and the whimsical and cruel autocrat of later years.

When they realized whither he had been leading them it was too late to withdraw. Those who tried to do so perished together with Stalin's old adversaries. Others suppressed their qualms, pretended to be in complete agreement with Stalin, and acted as he wished them to act. A man of great political ambition, seeing that all opposition was quixotic, might so manœuvre as to place himself in a position of influence, and gain a limited freedom to act according to his own principles, or, at any rate, to contribute effectively to the progressive aspects of Stalin's policy. If he was, like Malenkov, young enough to survive Stalin, such a man could even hope that one day he would be able to use his influence to undo some of the things done under Stalin, and perhaps even to bring back to the Soviet State the humane socialist spirit of its early days. There was in the Stalinist lingo a special term for such men: *dvurushniki*, the double-faced. Was Malenkov perhaps a *dvurushnik*?

This may be too charitable an interpretation of his behaviour under Stalin. It is more probable that until very late in the day he had no mental reservations at all, and that he was indeed, as the world had known him, the most devoted and fanatical of Stalin's assistants. All the more remarkable would his conduct then appear after Stalin's death, for it would underline the fact that Russia's urge to shake off the worst of Stalinism had

become so strong that it compelled Stalin's arch-devotee
to become the liquidator of the Stalin era.

An analogy to this situation may be found in what
happened in Russia during the last years of the reign of
Nicholas I, the Iron Tsar (1825–55), and during the first
years of his successor Alexander II (1855–81).

Nicholas I was the most tyrannical of the Tsars of
the nineteenth century. The last period of his reign,
writes an historian of Russia, 'was one of complete suffo-
cation'. The universities were placed under the strictest
police surveillance. The teaching of some subjects was
completely forbidden. Philosophy could be taught only
as part of Divinity. Even the most loyal Slavophiles were
savagely persecuted. Newspapers were forbidden to
report new inventions until it was officially declared that
they were useful. A special commission examined all
music to ensure that no conspiratorial code was concealed
in it. The censorship banned expressions like 'forces of
nature' or 'the movement of ideas'. But the greatest
crime of all was to discuss the main social problem agita-
ting Russia—the peasants' serfdom. The Tsar was determined to preserve serfdom intact.

Under Nicholas I 'hypocrisy permeated Russian
society from top to bottom', writes another historian.
The Tsar set the example. When a Siberian governor
proposed capital punishment for a gang of criminals, the
Tsar commented on the governor's report: 'The death
penalty has been, thank God, abolished in Russia; and
it is not for me to restore it. Let every one of the bandits
be given 12,000 lashes.' (The strongest man could not
survive more than 3,000 strokes.) All affairs of State
were wrapped in deep secrecy. The budget was never
published; only the Tsar and a few Ministers knew its
contents. It was a grave offence for any official to divulge
even the most trivial fact. Herzen was banished from

Petersburg because in a letter to his father he described an incident in the street in which a policeman killed a passer-by. 'It was this hypocrisy . . . which made the reign of Nicholas I peculiarly oppressive. . . . When Nicholas died even his closest collaborators realized the necessity for a change.' But to the end the Tsar repeated: 'My successor may do as he pleases; for myself I cannot change.'

'My successor may do as he pleases; for myself I cannot change' might have been Stalin's last dictum as well.

That Alexander II would bring about any change in his father's system of government was as little expected as it was in our day that Malenkov would in any way depart from Stalinism. The new Tsar had been greatly attached and entirely loyal to his father, although it was believed that his tutor had inculcated a more liberal spirit. Alexander shared his father's narrow conservatism and barrack-square tastes. As heir-presumptive he had taken a prominent part in framing the most repressive measures. On several occasions he defended the interests of the serf-owners even more zealously than Nicholas. 'In the most reactionary period of the reign, after 1848, Alexander was almost prepared to go further than Nicholas.'

Yet no sooner had Alexander ascended the throne than he initiated a series of quasi-liberal reforms and began to prepare for the abolition of serfdom. When the dismayed nobility implored him to keep to his father's ways, Alexander replied: 'It is better to abolish serfdom from above than to wait till it begins to abolish itself from below.'

No immediate threat of a revolution from below was appnaret, however. There were no effective, articulate centres of opposition capable of leadership in such a revolution. The broad classes of Russian society were not ready for political action: they were prepared to go on living under autocratic rule. Accustomed to leave all

political initiative to the Imperial Court, they continued
to place all their hopes on the Court. But these hopes
were clear and insistent enough to impel the new Tsar
on the road of reform. Abolition of serfdom became a
national necessity—for under the old system Russia's
economic and social life was sinking into a morass of
irrationality. The supreme need of the time harnessed to
its service the man who as heir presumptive seemed
firmly to have set his face against it.

The analogy between the Russia of 1855 and that of
1953 is made here with all necessary reservations and
with appreciation of the differences in the social background and in Russia's position in the world. The epoch
of Nicholas I was one of economic and social stagnation,
although it was also characterized by an intense, largely
latent, movement of ideas within a very narrow circle of
the intelligentsia. The Stalin epoch was one of unprece-
dented economic and social progress. Despite the abolition of serfdom, the Russia of Alexander II was also
stagnant economically, which is not likely to be the case
with Russia after Stalin.

Yet, within limits, the similarities between the two
periods are undeniable. By the end of the Stalin era
Russian society was so accustomed to leaving all political initiative to its rulers that it had become incapable of
independent action. Reform could be initiated only from
above, from inside the ruling group. As one analyses
Malenkov's first moves, one can almost hear him pleading
in the inner circle of the Kremlin: *Better to abolish the
worst features of Stalinism from above than to wait until
they are abolished from below.*

CHAPTER EIGHT

AN ERA OF REFORM?

MALENKOV'S government began its work with the solemn assurance that it would preserve the continuity of Stalin's policy, both domestic and foreign.

What substance was there in that assurance?

Stalin's successors are committed to preserve and to develop further the broad lines of his economic and social policies. They are undoubtedly determined to forge ahead with industrialization. They will seek to enhance the collectivist structure of farming. They will adhere to planned economy. In other words, they will pursue the broad objectives of socialism, as understood by the Communist Party.

In these fundamental respects, therefore, their assurances of continuity need to be taken at least as seriously as Stalin's similar assurances after Lenin's death. Early in the Stalin era there still existed the material-economic, if not the political, possibility of a counter-revolution which might have restored capitalism. Private ownership still dominated rural economy and had important footholds in urban economy as well. Trotsky accused Stalin of paving the way for such a restoration by furthering the interests of the NEP bourgeoisie and the *kulaks*. Yet it was Stalin who suppressed both. In present-day Russia there exists no material-economic basis for any sort of restoration. It may be said that it was the broad historical function of Stalinism to bring about this state of affairs. Now, not merely the intentions of Stalin's successors nor even the use of political force, but the force of circumstances guarantees the continuity of the present economic order.

However, this is perhaps the only respect in which Malenkov's assertion of continuity was not hollow. In other respects the beginnings of a break with the Stalin era could be discerned in all the moves made by Malenkov's government in the first month of its existence.[1]

The Stalin cult began to wither as soon as its object had disappeared. Even the funeral orations, made by Malenkov, Beria, and Molotov on March 9th, for all their praise of the dead man, sounded strangely like an anti-climax to the shrill glorification which had surrounded the man while he lived. By the standards of the Stalinist liturgy, with its strict gradations of worship, the funeral eulogies were so subdued and perfunctory that the discerning ear could detect in them a hint almost of blasphemy. Malenkov made far fewer genuflexions than Stalin had made at Lenin's bier; and there was on this occasion no 'We swear to Thee, Comrade Stalin'. Instead, Malenkov devoted most of his speech to a succinct and sober *exposé* of governmental policy.

Even before this, on March 6th, only a few hours after Stalin's death, a decision was taken which to those familiar with the peculiar symbolism of the Stalin era was in a way more meaningful than a whole series of formal political resolutions. It was decreed that the Lenin Mausoleum, that central shrine of Stalinist Russia, be abolished and that a Pantheon be erected where the remains of Lenin and Stalin would be deposited. This decision was not merely a blow at the primitive magic of Stalinism—it indicated a desire to put an end to the Leader cult and to emphasize in a more civilized and rational manner the collective merits of the party. The decree stated that the Pantheon would receive, together with the coffins of Lenin and Stalin, the ashes of all those leaders and heroes of the revolution who had been interred at the Kremlin Wall in the Red Square and

[1] These lines were written at the beginning of April 1953.

whose names had remained in obscurity during the years of the Stalin cult. Malenkov's government could have made no more expressive gesture before Stalin's body was even carried down into the vault.

Also within a few hours of Stalin's decease a most sweeping reorganization of party and government was announced. The Præsidium of the party, elected with so much flourish only four months earlier, was reduced to about a third of its size. Fourteen Ministries were merged into five (and the merging continued at such a feverish rate that by March 15th forty-five Ministries had been reduced to fourteen).

In the distribution of offices some members of the Old Stalin Guard, Molotov and Shvernik, suffered veiled or open demotion, while others, Voroshilov and Kaganovich, who had been semi-eclipsed during Stalin's last years, gained promotion. In addition, Marshal Zhukov, the conqueror of Berlin, whom Stalin had kept in obscurity since 1946, was brought back as Deputy Minister of Defence.

A curious change took place in the Presidency of the Republic. Shvernik, Chairman of the Supreme Soviet and titular Head of State, and Gorkin, Secretary of the Supreme Soviet, were 'recommended' for dismissal or demotion; and Marshal Voroshilov was 'recommended' for the post of the new Head of State. Malenkov, as Prime Minister, was flanked by four Deputies: Beria, the head of the now merged Ministries of Internal Affairs and State Security; Molotov, Minister of Foreign Affairs; Marshal Bulganin, Minister of Defence; and Kaganovich, controller of all economic departments.

Events soon began to show the meaning of these changes. Their purpose was to concentrate power and control in the ruling group; but they also reflected a tug-of-war inside that group.

The swift and radical reshuffling of the leading personnel in party and government was officially explained on the ground that it was designed to assert unity of leadership and continuity of policy. At the March session of the Supreme Soviet Malenkov claimed that the merger of the Ministries had been planned long before in agreement with Stalin. He made no such claim, however, about the reorganization of the party leadership and the changes in the Presidency of the Republic.

Yet the structure of party leadership, as Malenkov found it on his accession, was generally believed to have been the proud work of Stalin himself, carried out in the last months of his life. On the eve of Malenkov's appointment, it was still hailed as a great feat beneficial to the party and conducive to a further increase in its strength and cohesiveness. The sudden undoing of that 'feat' suggested that Stalin's successors were throwing overboard his ideas on party organization.

Even more puzzling, in a way, was the change in the Presidency. Under the Soviet Constitution, the titular Head of State acts only as the Chairman of a collective body, called the Præsidium of the Supreme Soviet; he does not usually exercise great political influence. But in an *interregnum*, such as followed Stalin's death, his position is crucial, at least momentarily. According to constitutional usage, Shvernik and Gorkin, the Chairman and the Secretary of the Præsidium, should have put their signatures to the decree appointing Malenkov as Prime Minister and authorizing the other changes in the government. Yet the decree appeared under the anonymous collective signature of the Præsidium; and both Shvernik and Gorkin were demoted.

The signs of the demotion were unmistakable. At Stalin's funeral Shvernik could be seen only behind the far end of the group of leaders assembled at the Lenin Mausoleum. Yet nominally he was still President of the Republic since the instalment of Voroshilov was not to take place until a week later, at the session of the Supreme Soviet of March 15th. At that session Khrushchev introduced Voroshilov on behalf of the party with an eloquent eulogy, extolling the great merits and qualities which made the Marshal a most suitable candidate for the Presidency. Not a single kind word was said about the departing holder of the office—his services did not receive even the most perfunctory acknowledgment. Shvernik was voted out of the Presidency in icy silence.

It is difficult to believe that all this was a matter of chance; and that barely a few hours after Stalin's demise Shvernik had to leave the Presidency simply in order to become Chairman of the Trade Unions Council, as was officially announced. Was it perhaps that during the brief *interregnum*, Shvernik and Gorkin tried to use their constitutional prerogatives against Malenkov or against the sweeping overhaul of the ruling group? And that this was the real reason for their demotion?

Whichever is true, these changes were hardly calculated to lend support to the professions of continuity. Their cumulative effect may well have been to create a feeling that there was a strong, self-assured, new hand at the helm; but they also suggested that the statements about continuity need not be taken literally. Indeed, they provoked a sense of discontinuity and uncertainty among the Soviet hierarchy—and in public opinion as well. At the very moment of his accession Malenkov appeared to have carried out a triple *coup*—in the party, in the government, and in the Presidency. It was only natural that people should wonder about its implications.

About the time of Stalin's death—this much is obvious now—the reformers and the die-hard supporters of Stalinism were arrayed against one another. Through the changes in the party, the government, and the Presidency, the reformers strove to gain the upper hand.

At this point we pass from the analysis of basic trends in Soviet society to a view of the mechanics of political power.

The two material instruments of power on which the

regime relied in the past were: police and army. Both were controlled by the party, but each naturally had its distinctive outlook, its sectional interests, its policies and ambitions. The attitude of the army will be discussed later—here we are concerned with the part of the political police in the new situation.

The political police would not be true to character if it did not view with apprehension and suspicion any attempt to liberalize the regime. It has a vested interest in preserving the *status quo*. It has its spokesmen in the leading bodies of the party; and these must have warned the reformers that the experiments envisaged were dangerous and fraught with incalculable consequences. (Such Court struggles between gendarmes and semi-liberal reformers are not unusual in autocratic regimes; and in Russia they have recurred at every major political crisis.)

This is not to say that in the inner councils of the party Beria necessarily represented the 'anti-liberal' attitude of the police. He was called in by Stalin in 1939 to take over from Yezhov the direction of the N.K.V.D., to wind up the great purges and tame the political police whom Stalin himself had previously encouraged to run amok. Rightly or wrongly, Beria gained the reputation of being one of the more moderate and educated men in Stalin's entourage. As Minister of Internal Affairs he does not seem to have exercised direct control over the political police in recent years. The latter was managed by the Minister of State Security, and its last chief, Ignatiev, was responsible among other things for concocting the 'doctors' plot'.

The political police could hardly have been alone in its opposition to reform. Almost certainly it had its allies among Stalin's Old Guard, which was, and perhaps still is, divided on this issue. From conviction or from personal resentment at Malenkov's ascendancy, Molotov certainly looked askance at Malenkov's liberal gestures. The demoted Shvernik has for long been Molotov's close

I

associate; he headed the trade unions at the time when the unions helped to enforce a state of martial law in industry. By elevating Voroshilov to the Presidency and Kaganovich to the post of Vice-Premier responsible for the conduct of economic affairs, Malenkov evidently set two members of the Old Guard against Molotov and Shvernik.

Malenkov's first preoccupation was to keep the political police in check and to prevent its interference with contemplated reforms. As early as March 6th he merged the Ministry of State Security with that of Internal Affairs and placed Beria at the head of the united department. Ignatiev, the last Minister of State Security, was transferred to the Secretariat of the Party a week later, on March 14th. In the light of subsequent events this appointment appears to have been calculated to confound the die-hards in the political police. They were evidently led to believe that as one of the five new Party Secretaries Ignatiev would be able to counteract effectively the reformist trend. In the meantime Beria acted, opened the dossiers of the former Ministry of State Security, and investigated the background to the 'doctors' plot'.

At the same session of the Central Committee at which Ignatiev was assigned to the General Secretariat of the Party, Malenkov resigned from it. If we are to believe the official account, Malenkov himself asked to be relieved from the Secretariat in order to be able to devote his undivided attention to government affairs. It is possible, of course, that Malenkov did not weaken his position by surrendering his post at the Secretariat. The Secretariat may not be as important to him as it once was to Stalin: unlike Stalin, Malenkov was able to place his supporters at all the levers of the party machine long before his assumption of power. Alternatively, Malenkov may have withdrawn from the Secretariat under pressure from opponents who were jealous of his holding all the highest offices in both party and State. What indicates that there was friction and bargaining on this point is the circumstance that Malenkov's resignation, allegedly decided on March 14th, was not announced until a week later, on March 21st.

The adherents of reform scored their first signal success with the announcement of an amnesty on March 28th. The amnesty may have been the result of a compromise. But the terms in which it was presented and, even more, the motives given for it appear to have been designed to disgrace the political police and—by implication—the dead Stalin.

'Vigilance!' had been the time-honoured battle cry of the political police. The argument for vigilance had run: Although socialism was triumphant in the Soviet Union and the old property-owning classes had vanished, the class struggle continued unabated; the very progress of socialism was driving foreign and domestic enemies to extremes of sabotage, treachery, and terrorism.

The reformers did not, of course, deny the need for vigilance; but they placed the emphasis on the strength and consolidation of the Soviet regime, and on the growing socialist maturity of the people, which made a more lenient policy both possible and necessary.

These shifts of emphasis were reflected even in the Soviet Press. Some writers argued: Yes, we are stronger, *but* the need for vigilance is greater than ever. Others reversed the argument: Yes, we need vigilance, *but* we are stronger than ever.

We *are* stronger than ever and therefore we can afford leniency—said the preamble to the decree of amnesty, without so much as a mention of 'vigilance'.

The terms of the amnesty were remarkable in many respects.

For the first time the government officially told the world that there had been in the prisons and concentration camps mothers with children, pregnant women, sick and old people, and boys and girls under eighteen.

All convicts of these categories were released, regardless of the nature of their offence and the terms of their sentence. All other convicts sentenced to less than five years also regained freedom. The sentences of those serving more than five years were reduced by half. The excluded were counter-revolutionaries, embezzlers of very large sums, and bandits guilty of murder. The amnesty applied to military as well as civilian convicts. All prosecutions for offences covered by the decree immediately ceased.

Perhaps the most striking feature of the amnesty was that it restored civil rights to all those released under its terms, and also to those who had served their sentences and had been released before the amnesty. Thus the old principle 'once a criminal always a criminal', a principle by which no Soviet citizen who had once been in the hands of the political police could ever again become a free man, was abandoned.

The decree left one point vague: it did not define who were the counter-revolutionaries excluded from pardon. All the same, the amnesty must have resulted in the closing down of many or most of the concentration camps. Among the inmates of those camps the majority were people sentenced to not more than five years; and in recent times very few seem to have been convicted for counter-revolution. But hitherto the terms of a sentence had often been meaningless: after the lapse of five years, the political police could 'administratively' detain the convict for a further term. The amnesty apparently also put an end to this barbarous practice.

The deeper moral implications of the act were most significant. In the hearing of the whole of Russia and of the world Malenkov's government said in effect to the released prisoners:

'You have suffered innocently, you pregnant women, you mothers and children, you boys and girls under eighteen, you the old and the sick, and all the rest of you!

'It was Stalin who needlessly kept you behind bars and barbed wire, and who deprived you of civil rights.

We have no need for such barbarity. *We* are releasing you. Remember to whom you owe your freedom.'

Perhaps Malenkov and his associates did not want to intimate as much as that. Perhaps they only sought to gain popularity. But this is how Russia was bound to understand the message of the amnesty. No more telling blow could be dealt to the Stalin cult.

To underline the fact that a new era was being inaugurated, the decree of amnesty also foreshadowed a revision of the criminal codes. True, there had been talk of this even while Stalin was still alive. But it had never been made clear in what spirit the revision was to be carried out. Evidently this too was a bone of contention between the reformers and their adversaries.

The decree of March 28th stated that the new codes would abolish criminal responsibility for minor offences committed by officials, industrial managers, workers, and collective farmers. They would also reduce punishment for a variety of other offences. Thus a promise was made to abolish or soften the harsh martial discipline that had prevailed in factories and collective farms during nearly two decades. This was no mere gesture of magnanimity on the part of a new government seeking popularity. The reform would be in line with the new outlook of the Soviet economy which no longer requires that millions of uprooted and illiterate peasants be forcibly trained in the industrial way of life. The old discipline that furthered Russia's economic development at one time has now become an obstacle to it.

Altogether the implications of the decree of March 28th were so far-reaching as to permit us to describe that day as the birth date of a new regime.

Another week had scarcely passed before, on April 3rd and 4th, the political police was subjected to devastating humiliation. Its latest feat of vigilance, the 'discovery' of the 'doctors' plot', was exposed before Russia and the whole world as a criminal fraud. A certain Riumin, chief of the Investigation Department in the former Ministry of State Security, was named as the official responsible for the concoction. He was arrested. A woman informer, Doctor Timashuk, who had helped to arraign the Kremlin physicians and had been awarded for this the Order of Lenin and been celebrated as a national heroine, was deprived of the Order and disgraced.

Three days later, on April 6th, Ignatiev, the former Minister of State Security, so recently elected to the General Secretariat of the Party, was dismissed with ignominy from his new post. At the same time the government firmly disavowed the campaign of anti-Semitic insinuation and incitement which had been waged since the alleged discovery of the doctors' conspiracy.

If this had been all, the event would have been startling, but it would not necessarily have signified a dramatic break with the Stalin era. Under Stalin too, Russia had seen chiefs of the G.P.U. or N.K.V.D., masters of life and death, suddenly dismissed in disgrace. One of them, Yagoda, was even tried and executed as a 'traitor' and 'enemy of the people'. But such occurrences were merely incidents in the great purges; and we now know that Yagoda was victimized because he had shown himself reluctant and half-hearted in arraigning the old Bolsheviks. Up to 1939 the political police was purged only in order to force it to intensify the purges. This was obviously not the motive behind the dismissal of Ignatiev and Riumin. The political police was now 'purged' in order to prevent it from starting a new series of frame-ups.

This was shown clearly by the manner in which the Kremlin physicians were rehabilitated. The government declared that the political police had extorted the evidence against them 'by methods which were inadmissible and strictly forbidden by Soviet law'. In other words, the police had forced the doctors to make confessions in line with those that had figured so strangely and prominently in every purge trial and invariably had provided the only 'evidence' for the prosecution.

It should be pointed out that in 1939, when Beria was winding up the purges, many of the victims were also released and even rehabilitated. This was done on the ground that the accusations had been 'based on a deplorable misunderstanding'—these words became a routine formula at the time. Never during the Stalin era was the political police charged with illegal extortion of evidence. Never was the secret of the 'confessions' officially and publicly exposed.

It was on those 'confessions' that the omnipotence of the police rested. Their regularity, their inevitability, and their nightmarish character had invested the political police with a mysterious power, a basilisk look, which no Soviet citizen could hope to withstand or elude. No matter how innocent he might be of the crimes attributed to him, the citizen knew that he was helpless and would not be allowed to prove his innocence. Subjected to ceaseless day-and-night 'interrogation' over weeks and months he was sure to reach the limits of endurance, to collapse and confess, and thus supply his persecutors with the 'evidence' they needed. In recent years this technique was not frequently applied in Russia, although it was readily exported to Czechoslovakia, Hungary, and Bulgaria. But as long as the technique was not officially and publicly exposed the mainspring of the machinery of terror remained intact.

At that mainspring Malenkov's government struck a telling blow when it ordered the arrest of the officials who had been in charge of the investigation into the 'doctors' plot', and when it publicly exposed the criminal manner in which they had extorted their 'evidence'.

Officials who had the extraction of 'confessions' on their conscience must have read with a shudder the communiqué about the release of the Kremlin physicians. The shudder must have been felt in every dark office of the political police throughout Russia. Every man, high and low, in the service must have wondered whether, if he ever again tried to extort confessions, he would not be made to pay for it with his head or at least his freedom. The masters of terror were themselves terrified, and the mass of the Soviet people must have been thrilled by the mere thought that henceforth they might be free to defend their rights against their persecutors. Malenkov's government explicitly assured them of this.

It was as if a long, severe, cruel political winter was over, a Siberian winter which had lasted for more than two decades. Spring was in the air; and, politically, the whole of Russia seemed to be clearing the snow from her doorsteps in those memorable April days.

Great historical changes in the climate of a country sometimes show themselves more directly in ordinary scenes of daily life than in the official documents, public statements and pompous editorials, from which an unimaginative historian will one day construe a dead picture of those days. The official documents and even—who would have supposed it?—the editorials of *Pravda* made exciting reading. But they conveyed little in comparison, for instance, with this description of a seemingly trivial street incident given by Mr. Knudson, one of a group of American journalists who visited Moscow early in April.

'To the amazement of Western nationals in Moscow and the Russians themselves, the Americans were allowed to use their cameras freely.' Under the Stalinist obsession with secrecy this was unthinkable. Yet the ban on the use of cameras was not rescinded. Mr. Knudson himself was stopped in Moscow by a policeman when he was taking photographs and was asked to produce his passport. 'I left my passport at the hotel, and as the policeman tried to talk to me in Russian a large crowd gathered. One of the Russians was a woman who spoke English. I told her I was one of the visiting newspaper men. "Let him go. He is an American," she told the policeman. And he did.' (The *Manchester Guardian*, 10 April 1953.)

This little scene in which a policeman, disregarding his standing orders and instructions, did what a woman from the crowd told him to do, sums up the new mood.

But can Malenkov's government afford to destroy the mainspring of the terror? Dare he throw out of gear the whole machinery of terror?

Malenkov almost certainly intends to tame rather than to undo the political police. It is always difficult and dangerous for any dictatorial regime to try to liberalize itself. Popular grievances pent up in previous years may be so intense and bitter that, once the floodgates are thrown open, the grievances may overflow and threaten all groups associated with the previous regime, including the reformers.

The reformers may then take fright, shrink from the consequences of their own liberal gestures, and surrender to the adherents of the terror.

Up to the middle of April 1953 no sign of such a development had become visible. However, popular reaction against the old terror may assume a less direct, less political character. It may show itself in a spontaneous slackening of social discipline, in particular of labour discipline; a slackening which could disturb the national economy and the rhythm of its work. The government might then feel tempted, or be driven, to curtail the freedoms it had just granted. An inclination to show the strong arm once again would not be surprising in men trained in the Stalin school of government. Malenkov and his associates are still half submerged in their Stalinist past even though they attempt to escape from it.

Nor is it certain that Malenkov's government is quite aware of the far-reaching implications of its own deeds.

Under the amnesty civil rights have been restored to the survivors of the great purges. They may be a mere handful, but they will speak of their experiences and record them. Some may even take courage and ask for an open and formal revision of their cases. Whether they do so or not, history has in any case already begun a great revision of the purge trials. Russia's mind has been set in motion. When the people are told that the political police trumped up charges and forced defendants to confess imaginary crimes, disturbing questions must begin to stir in many minds:

Was the case of the Kremlin doctors exceptional? Were the previous trials not also based on frame-ups? Were Zinoviev, Kamenev, Bukharin, Radek, Tukhachevsky, Rykov, and so many other former heroes of the revolution really guilty of the crimes attributed to them? Were they spies, terrorists, traitors? Or did they die as martyrs? Should not perhaps their ashes too be interred in the Pantheon? Should not the remains of Trotsky be brought back from remote Mexico and laid to rest there? Should not the archives be thrown open to reveal the whole inner story of the past and fix the responsibility for its horrors?

Such doubts will now inevitably, though perhaps slowly, invade the minds of the intelligentsia and the workers.

Malenkov's government may be anxious to put an end to the misdeeds of the political police and to restore the constitutional rights of the people. But it also has a vested interest in preventing or delaying a historic revision of the old purges. It wishes to manage the present more rationally, but it can have no desire to throw a rational light on the past, in which all its members were implicated, some more and others less. (Vyshinsky, the chief prosecutor in all purge trials and the detestable author of the worst frame-ups, still represents Malenkov's government at the United Nations.)

It is even doubtful whether the government can afford

to give a fair trial to the officials charged with fabricating the 'doctors' plot'. Such a trial might lead to most embarrassing revelations. The defendants might plead mitigating circumstances and point to accomplices and instigators higher up. They might try to explain a few curious details of the fabrication and wittingly or unwittingly bring to light deeper cleavages in the State which have perhaps not yet been overcome.

If, to avoid such embarrassing consequences, the trial were to be staged in the familiar style, with set speeches and confessions, then its result would be merely to make scapegoats of a few officials, to reduce to a mockery Malenkov's assurances about the new era of constitutional rights, and to restore the arbitrary powers of the political police. It would therefore not be surprising if, to escape the dilemma, the government either avoided a *public* trial altogether or under some pretext delayed it indefinitely.

In any case it is still possible that a new gust of cold Siberian wind will nip the first shoots of reform, and that the hopeful opening of a new era will be followed by disillusionment.

Once again the phantoms of 1855 and 1861 may return to the Russian scene.

When Alexander II initiated the 'liberal era' even the most extreme opponents of Tsardom acclaimed him with enthusiasm. Herzen and Chernyshevsky, the two leaders of radical and revolutionary opinion, hailed the Emancipator. The new era was no mere wishful dream. Russian peasants were serfs no longer. Censorship practically ceased, although it was not formally abolished. Restrictions on the freedom of movement of Russian subjects, especially the ban on travelling abroad which had been enforced by Nicholas I, were declared null and void. Every kind of official abuse was exposed, and the old reactionary civil service was disgraced. In one of his first proclamations Alexander stated in words not very different from those that Malenkov has now used: 'May Russia's internal welfare be established and perfected; may justice and mercy reign in her Law Courts.'

But the system of government remained autocratic, and presently Alexander found that the leaders of opinion demanded more freedom than he was prepared to grant. He began to hesitate and to retrace his steps. And as he attempted to reimpose despotism he aroused poignant disillusionment. Chernyshevsky was convicted to hard labour and deported. Even before that Herzen had become doubtful. On the evening in 1861 when he invited friends to his London home to celebrate the emancipation of the Russian peasants, he learned about the bloody suppression of Polish demonstrations. He raised his glass to drink the Tsar's health, but interrupted himself to say: 'Friends, our day of rejoicing is darkened by unexpected news: blood is flowing in Warsaw.'

How far is Malenkov prepared to go on the road of reform?

The members of the ruling group can hardly see eye to eye on this issue. There are among them the men of Stalin's Old Guard who were prominently associated with the terror of previous years; and there are also the representatives of the younger generation who are freer to promote reform. But to carry out a complete revision of the Stalin era men may be needed even younger than those for whom Malenkov speaks, men with no stake at all in Stalinist orthodoxy.

CHAPTER NINE

FUTURE PROSPECTS: FOREIGN POLICY

I N his first statement as Prime Minister, Malenkov said:

'The most correct, indispensable, and just foreign policy is a policy of peace between all peoples, a policy of mutual confidence, business-like, based on facts, and confirmed by facts.'

Malenkov's words were an implicit criticism of Stalin's conduct of foreign affairs, although the criticism applied to the manner rather than the matter of Stalinist diplomacy.

Stalin's foreign policy was bogged down in the irrationalism of the cult and the magic. His diplomacy did not lack a peculiar realism and shrewdness; but it was incapable of facing facts. It was obsessed with prestige. Nothing could be allowed to detract from the greatness and infallibility of the Father of the Peoples. Every Soviet success had to be fantastically exaggerated; every reverse had to be dressed up as a success. Not only propagandists, but also ambassadors and diplomatic spokesmen had to conform to this style. Consequently the hypocrisy which permeated domestic policy affected foreign policy also; and this hypocrisy accounted for the bizarre unreality and rigidity in Stalinist diplomacy.

To be sure, in critical situations Stalin carried out sharp reversals of policy which gave the impression of great flexibility. But the need for these sudden and sharp reversals sprang also from rigidity. Quick perception of shifts in international alignments, the subtle nuance and manœuvre, the gradual transition from one policy to another—all these were beyond Stalin's diplomacy. Instructed to pursue a certain line of conduct, Soviet Foreign Ministers followed their instructions to the point of absurdity, until Stalin himself suddenly stopped them and ordered them to turn in the opposite direction.

At home a quotation from Stalin was supposed to resolve any doubt on any subject. Therefore the final and decisive argument produced by Vyshinsky, Malik, and Gromyko before hostile or indifferent foreign audiences was also the sacred quotation from Stalin. Even when they had a strong case to make they most often wrecked it through unbusiness-like presentation. They had to repeat *ad nauseam* the same abuses or protestations of friendship, regardless of the situation.

Stalinist propaganda usually vaunted the agility of Soviet diplomacy in exploiting 'the contradictions in the enemy camp'; and anti-Stalinists believed in this and feared it. In fact, Stalin's diplomacy frequently acted as if it were desperately anxious to eliminate all those 'contradictions in the bourgeois camp': it semed bent on uniting adversaries and on turning neutrals into adversaries. If it, nevertheless, benefited from divisions in the anti-communist world, this was due to the inherent force of those divisions.

Malenkov's first preoccupation was to free Soviet foreign policy from its irrational Byzantinism and to make it more worldly and subtle. A peace policy 'based on facts' required that Soviet diplomacy relax its inflexible attitudes and postures. Such a policy could not be pursued by means of constant repetition of clichés dictated by requirements of domestic orthodoxy but utterly ineffective or even incomprehensible when produced at an international forum.

Almost immediately after Stalin's funeral, the style of Soviet diplomacy became more civilized and sober. Less obsessed with prestige than its predecessor, Malenkov's government proceeded to free itself from some of the rigid commitments it had inherited. It dealt in a conciliatory spirit with incidents in the 'air corridor' from Western Germany to Berlin. It offered its services in repatriating British and French civilian prisoners from Korea. It ceased to obstruct the election of a new General Secretary of the United Nations. In these gestures of conciliation there was no surrender of any vital Soviet interest. But even if only gestures, they contrasted refreshingly with the ceaseless mutual mud-slinging of the cold war.

Soon afterwards, on March 28th, the Chinese and North Koreans—under Soviet inspiration—made new proposals for armistice negotiations in Korea. The previous protracted negotiations had reached a deadlock over one point: the repatriation of prisoners of war. With Soviet support, the North Koreans and Chinese had insisted on the unconditional repatriation of all their prisoners. Now they announced that they were willing to abandon that demand.

The new Soviet attitude over the Korean war was no mere change in diplomatic style—it foreshadowed a new policy.

It is evident that during Stalin's last years the ruling circles were divided over foreign policy at least as much as over domestic affairs. This division was not very different from that familiar in other countries. One faction was anxious to seek conciliation with the West, another refused to countenance 'appeasement'. There is no need to have recourse to guesswork in order to reconstruct the broad outlines of the disagreement—Stalin himself provided the clue in his much discussed *Bolshevik* article on the eve of the Nineteenth Party Congress.

The disagreement was logically premissed on two opposite views about the prospects of war and peace.

One group held that war between a united capitalist world and the communist bloc was 'inevitable'; and that it was probably inevitable in the near future. The other group took the view that accommodation between the two camps was still possible and even probable, despite mounting tension.

This controversy directly affected the Soviet attitude over Germany and Korea, the two main storm centres of world politics.

The opponents of 'appeasement' refused to consider any compromise with the West over Germany and Austria. They refused, in the first instance, to contemplate the prospect of a Soviet military withdrawal from Central Europe. If, as they held, a new world war was inevitable and near, then it was obviously in the Soviet interest to hold on to all advanced strategic outposts on the Elbe and the Danube. These outposts were equally vital in offensive and defensive operational plans. They could be used as jumping-off grounds for an advance into Western Europe; and they could serve as shock absorbers in case of a Western attack. From this viewpoint, Moscow was interested in preserving the *status quo*, in keeping Germany divided until the outbreak of war, and in completely integrating Eastern Germany in the Soviet bloc. All talk about Germany's unification was empty propaganda.

The conciliators recognized, of course, the advantage of holding Eastern Germany. But almost certainly they argued that if Russia could buy peace and a long breathing spell at the price of a withdrawal from Germany and Austria, she ought to pay that price. Germany's reunification should be the major aim of Soviet policy, not a propaganda stunt. Reunification might entail the loss of the communist regime in Eastern Germany. But Soviet Russia had more than once sold space to buy time, and she could do so again. Even from the conciliators' viewpoint, however, this concession to the West should be made only if, as a counterpart, the Western powers also agreed to withdraw their forces from Germany. A neutral Germany would be a useful buffer between East and West; but it was for Russia a matter of only secondary importance whether Germany freed from occupation would be neutral or remain a member of the European Defence Community. The edge of the European Defence Community would be blunted anyhow, and after the occupation armies had withdrawn a prolonged international *détente* could be expected.

The controversy affected Korea similarly. In the view of those who held world war to be inevitable and near, it was in the Soviet interest to prolong the fighting in Korea, to pin down as high a proportion as possible of American military power, and so to obstruct the building up in Europe of the military effectives and reserves of the Atlantic bloc. From the 'appeasers'' viewpoint the risks of prolonging the fighting were prohibitive. The Korean war provided a powerful stimulus to Western rearmament and the belligerent mood in the West; and it was more important for Russia to stop the armament race in time than to pin down American forces in the Far East.

This conflict of views was very close to the surface of Soviet foreign policy in recent years. Stalin personally placed on record his view that war between the communist and anti-communist blocs was neither 'inevitable' nor even probable. He agreed with the 'appeasers'' premiss but did not draw all the inferences from it. Acting, as usually, as supreme arbiter of the opposing factions, he avoided an explicit and final refutation of the views of either and delayed the ultimate decision until a critical moment.

In this way, Stalin imposed a stalemate on the two hostile factions and Soviet policy was the resultant of their conflicting views. This accounts for its peculiar indecisiveness and lack of direction. Geared neither to war nor to peace, the policy tried to pursue simultaneously the objectives of both. Nearly all Soviet diplo-

K

matic documents and pronouncements of recent years
were a patchwork of contradictory formulæ; and it is
easy to distinguish those designed to meet the views of
the conciliators from those calculated to satisfy their
opponents. Thus, Stalin's diplomacy repeatedly proposed the withdrawal of occupation armies from Germany; but it always appended conditions which from the
start made the proposals unacceptable to the Western
powers. Similarly, Moscow took the initiative for armistice negotiations in Korea, allowed all controversial issues
to be settled, but produced a 'hitch' over the last point
on the agenda. The conciliators in the Kremlin saw the
stage set for an armistice; and their opponents were
satisfied that a cease fire would not be sounded.

Who were the conciliators and who were their opponents?

According to Titoist sources, Malenkov headed the so-
called peace party. He had been opposed to the blockade
of Berlin in 1948; and he had repeatedly urged Stalin to
adopt a milder foreign policy. He was probably supported
by most of those who openly or tacitly favoured domestic
reform, because an easing of international tension was,
and still is, an essential condition for the success of
domestic reform.

While in domestic policy Malenkov had to fight the
die-hards of the security police, in foreign policy he had
to contend with the opposition of influential army
leaders. In Russia, as elsewhere, Chiefs of Staffs and
prospective commanders are concerned mainly with their
operational plans. They survey mentally the future
battlefields, inspect the outposts and ramparts; and they
are reluctant to give up any of these. In their eyes a conciliatory policy which would necessitate the withdrawal
of Soviet troops from the Elbe and the Danube and
allow American armed forces to disengage themselves
from Korea was too dangerous to contemplate.

Conceptions of foreign policy were thus mixed up with
the pros and cons of domestic reform; and both foreign

and domestic aspects were equally important in the last incident of the struggle before Stalin's death, the 'doctors' plot'.

The alleged discovery of the conspiracy in the Kremlin was designed to make domestic reform impossible. It was also calculated to inflict a blow at 'appeasement'. Its purpose was to create an atmosphere of war-like fever and nationalist hysteria, and to cut off the communist bloc from any contact with the West. In such a mood the 'alien', the citizen suspected of 'divided loyalties', is naturally regarded as the worst 'security risk', to use a current expression. And who could be a worse 'security risk' than the Jew with Zionist sympathies or the 'rootless cosmopolitan' whose brothers or cousins lived in the West?

There is circumstantial evidence that alongside officials of the political police some army leaders were also involved in the case of the doctors' plot. In that affair both scored a dramatic but indecisive success. Between the middle of January, when the tale about the Kremlin physicians was first published, and March, there were several indications that the struggle continued unabated behind the scenes. At the height of the anti-Jewish campaign two spectacular ceremonies were staged to honour two Jews. Mekhlis, former chief political commissar of the army, who had just died, was given an elaborate State funeral quite out of proportion to his official importance. Ilya Ehrenburg, the writer, was honoured with a high award and used the occasion to argue in public against racial discrimination. *Pravda* fully reported his speech, which it would hardly have done without orders from above.

At this stage Stalin may have been too ill to intervene, or else he kept himself *au dessus de la mêlée* and allowed the leaders of the opposing factions to do as they liked.

From Moscow the struggle had already spread to the provinces, and also abroad—to Prague, Warsaw, Budapest, and Bucharest. The two factions competed for control over the administrations of the satellite countries. This fact produced a curious diversity in the regimes of those countries and the methods employed by their Communist Parties.

The most striking contrast was between the Czech and the Polish scenes. In the Czech party a complete upheaval was carried out with lightning speed in 1952. Slansky, Clementis, and other prominent leaders were demoted and after only a few months executed as traitors, Zionists, Trotskyists, and foreign spies. The Slansky trial was a prelude to the spectacle that was to be enacted in Moscow; in both places the same hand pulled the wires. In Poland, G(mulka and his associates had been charged with 'nationalist deviation' as long ago as 1948. Yet for nearly five years no purge trial was staged. No accusation of terrorism, sabotage, or foreign espionage was added to the not unfounded charge of nationalism levelled against Gomulka. Nor has any other purge trial modelled on the Stalinist pattern taken place in Poland so far. Poland and possibly Rumania were obviously aligned with the conciliators and reformers in Moscow, while Czechoslovakia was swayed by their opponents, and in Hungary the two factions held each other in check. This state of affairs could last only as long as the struggle had not been resolved in Moscow.

On March 5th and 6th the 'peace party', led by Malenkov, carried out its *coup*, placed itself in power, and at once intimated its desire for an improvement in Russia's relations with the West.

The first moves which Malenkov's government made in this direction were relatively easy to take. The Soviet diplomatic envoys were instructed to speak softly. So were the Soviet newspapers. The Chinese and North Koreans were promptly persuaded to prepare for the winding up of the Korean war. Overnight they dropped their previous objection to 'voluntary repatriation' of prisoners of war, the objection on which the armistice negotiations had foundered.

These first moves made their impression in the West. But the real test of the new policy was, and at the time of writing is still, to come. Has the conflict between East and West not been allowed to drift too far to make a genuine easing of tension and conciliation extremely difficult or even impossible? Soft words are certainly not enough. The aggressive language in which East and West have spoken to one another aggravated the international tension, but it was not its major cause. A cease fire in Korea may bring about an improvement; but by itself it cannot solve the conflict of interests that led to the Korean war. Beyond Korea there remain the grave issues of control over armaments and of Germany and Austria. Over all these questions Russia and the Atlantic powers failed to find a common meeting ground during many years. Will they be able to find it now?

The domestic reforms already initiated in Russia strongly suggest that the new government is anxious to call a halt to the armament race. A Soviet regime freer than Stalin's needs for its survival firm popular support. It must therefore strive to raise the national standard of living; it must offer more butter and fewer guns.

Hitherto mutual fear and suspicion have dominated every debate on disarmament. The Western powers were apprehensive of Russia's superiority in 'conventional' arms; while Russia feared American superiority in atomic and other 'unconventional' weapons. Each camp hoped to redress the balance in its favour, Russia by accumulating a pile of atom bombs, and the United States by building up the armies of the Atlantic Alliance.

Of late there has been a feeling in each camp that it may not be able to 'redress the balance'. It is not known whether Russia's rulers had hoped to attain parity in atomic weapons with the United States in the foreseeable future. If so, recent American progress in that field must have caused sober reflection in the Kremlin. On the other hand, it has become apparent that the Atlantic powers had taken far too optimistic a view of their ability to raise joint armies which could counterbalance the armed strength of the Russian bloc in Europe and Asia. The armament race has reached a point at which each of the chief participants has reason to wonder whether he has much chance of winning.

Yet, while the results of the race so far may not have favoured either side, neither has seemed able to stop it. Each bloc would like the other to reduce its strength in those fields where it is superior. Russia has clamoured for the destruction of the atom bombs and for a ban on their use. The Western powers have demanded that Russia should first reduce her vast standing armies. Each side has been wondering just how great the other's superiority is. The West has pressed Russia to reveal the size of her armies; and Russia has asked about the size of the American stock of atomic weapons. Both have closely guarded their secrets and refused to divulge them, unless the other side sets the example first. And even if one side were to disclose its strength, the other would refuse to believe the truth of the disclosure, unless it was allowed to check it on the spot. Thus every debate has invariably led back to the question of 'international supervision and control'.

The history of this century is strewn with the wreckage of international conventions on disarmament; and it is extremely difficult to believe in the efficacy of new conventions. But it is possible that now, when Russia is moving away from the Stalin era, some of the old obstacles to agreement may vanish. As Russian obsession with secrecy lessens, a degree of conventional international supervision of armaments may become feasible. There has always been ground for the suspicion that what Stalin concealed so stubbornly from the world was not merely and perhaps not primarily the state of Russia's armaments but her low standard of living, her lack of freedom, and her concentration camps. Malenkov's government may be more inclined to allow United Nations commissions to travel inside Russia and inspect military establishments.

This, however, is the extreme limit to which it can go. Just as its predecessor, it will in no circumstances accept the demand for international ownership or management of the sources of atomic energy and of atomic plant. If the West insists on this, the deadlock over disarmament will continue. Even without this, the chances of agreement are slender enough. If Russia were to accept international supervision and inspection of military establishments, would the Western nations reciprocate? Obsession with military secrecy has recently grown so strong in the West as to justify scepticism on that point.

(It is one of the most tragi-comic developments of our day that the more intense the obsession with secrecy, the less effectively governments guard their secrets from their enemies. Stalin's most elaborate devices designed to cut off Russia from the West have not prevented multitudes of Soviet citizens from escaping and supplying Western Intelligence Services with a richer harvest of information than the most ingenious espionage network could collect. Western secrecy has not prevented Russia from obtaining the most closely guarded atomic secrets from the West's most competent scientists. But both East and West have paid for their mania of secrecy with a demoralization in government and people, with panic and witch-hunts.)

However, disarmament rarely if ever results from formal international conventions. It comes about spontaneously after a genuine *détente* has eased relations between great powers. Since the chief obstacle to such a *détente* lies in the problem of Germany and Austria, it is there that Malenkov's government is likely to seek a new solution.

The scope for new solutions, however, is extremely limited. Russia can probably do nothing more than re-

formulate her proposals for a withdrawal of the occupation armies and for unification of Germany.

The Western powers have so far rejected these
proposals for two reasons. Hitherto, because of the
tug-of-war in the Kremlin, the proposals have been
couched in terms that made them unacceptable from the
start. Russia suggested unification in the form of a merger
between the existing East and West German administrations. The Western powers naturally suspected that such
schemes concealed a Russian design for communist 'infiltration' of the whole of Germany; and they demanded
free elections in the Soviet Zone as a preliminary to
further agreement. If all German parties, including the
banned social democrats, were allowed to electioneer, the
communist government of Pieck and Ulbricht would
collapse. Until now Russia was not prepared to face this
consequence. A withdrawal of the occupation armies was
therefore out of the question.

This, however, has not been the sole reason for the
negative attitude of the Western powers on the unification of Germany. Equally important has been their fear
that the withdrawal of American forces would auto-
matically result in Russian predominance on the European continent. The United States would retire beyond
the Atlantic, while Soviet armed power would to all
intents and purposes remain on the Neisse and the Oder.

What can Malenkov's government do to break this
deadlock?

The possibility cannot be ruled out that in their desire to
resolve this potentially dangerous situation Russia's new
rulers may go so far as to permit free elections in the
Soviet zone, without attempting to save the communist
government there. The restoration of a bourgeois regime
in Eastern Germany is the highest price the Kremlin can
possibly agree to pay for the withdrawal of all occupation
armies. What must trouble the 'appeasers' in the Kremlin is whether they can secure a withdrawal even at that
price. After the instatement of a Christian Democratic or

Social Democratic government in the whole of Germany, will Western policy cease to be dominated by the fear of Russian predominance in Europe? In the long run Russia's proximity and growing industrial strength will most likely secure for her that predominance. This being the case and the consequence of geography and historical development, there is little or nothing that any Russian government, even the most 'peace loving', can do to reassure the West. At the most it can pledge itself not to use this position for military or direct political expansion. But will the Western powers have confidence in such a commitment, even if it is backed up by the restoration of a bourgeois regime in Eastern Germany?

We have said before that the general doctrine of foreign policy bequeathed by Stalin to his successors is one of 'self-containment' within the communist third of the world. The main difficulty in the application of this doctrine is that the communist third of the world has no clearly demarcated boundaries. The frontiers of the two power blocs overlap dangerously. Self-containment would logically require that the overlapping zones be eliminated.

Malenkov's government may be expected to explore the lines of retreat from Germany. But it can retreat only if the Western powers do the same. Should they refuse and the occupation armies hold on to their positions, Soviet diplomacy may still try to avoid new conflicts and seek conciliation within the unpropitious framework of a partitioned Germany. Peace would then depend on palliatives. However, the prolongation of the present state of affairs, with Soviet and Western armies facing each other across the Elbe, would from the start gravely handicap Malenkov's peace policy. The demarcation line across Germany would remain a potential front line; and on both its sides the perilous manœuvering for positions and outposts would continue.

Malenkov has staked his reputation and perhaps his future on the success of his peace overtures. Opposition to 'appeasement' is probably as strong in the inner councils of the Kremlin as it is in Washington, though it is not vocal. For the moment the conciliators have the upper hand and the opportunity to put their policies to the test. They have begun to 'dig a tunnel of friendship' from their end and have appealed to the statesmen of the West to do likewise. In the meantime the Soviet opponents of 'appeasement' stand in the background and watch the scene. Should Malenkov's policy fail, they may yet come dramatically to the fore and reverse the trend.

The changes in Russia will strongly affect the communist movements of other countries.

The quiet winding up of the Stalin cult is already having repercussions in the ranks of world communism, even though Stalinist leaders outside Russia were at first comically slow in realizing what was happening in Moscow.

The crumbling of Stalinist orthodoxy is sure to be followed by an intense ferment of ideas which may eventually transform the outlook of Communist Parties everywhere. Much depends on the extent to which the Soviet Communist Party evolves in a new direction. If the barrack-square discipline of Stalinism gives place to a freer regime, genuine and public controversy may be expected to develop in the ranks of the Russian party. It will then be impossible for most foreign Communist Parties to maintain their 'monolithic' character. Once they begin to discuss frankly their own policies, they may abandon the puppet-like attitude towards Russia which was their chief characteristic throughout the Stalin era. They may regain a certain independence of outlook and a measure of autonomy which would free them from the encumbrances of the past and greatly enhance their appeal.

Should, however, the era of reform come to a premature end in Russia then this process would be cut short in the foreign communist movements too; although even then those parties would have to search for an ideological substitute for Stalinism. In any case world communism finds itself at an historic crossroad.

Whatever evolutionary stages lie ahead, the link between world communism and Russia is not likely to be broken. The communist devotion to Russia as the pioneer and mainstay of the whole movement, may change its character. It may free itself from the taint of subservience and become more spontaneous and dignified than it has been hitherto.

Here again Russia's new rulers may be confronted by a difficult dilemma. If the communist bloc is to pursue a policy of self-containment and 'peaceful coexistence' with capitalism, its leaders may think it advantageous to prevent the further spread of communism which might endanger the *status quo*. Yet they may not be able to impose upon foreign Communist Parties the discipline under which Stalin kept them. They may not be in a position to dictate the policies and control every move of French, Italian, or Indo-Chinese communists. We have seen how first Tito and then Mao wrecked Stalin's policy of self-containment. Another Mao may rise in some corner of Asia or another Tito may reach out for power in some part of Europe, and wreck Malenkov's policy of self-containment as well. Even if the rulers of the communist bloc were to discourage new revolutions, as Stalin did, their background and tradition would compel them to identify themselves with every new communist regime emerging in any part of the world. And any such development would tend to aggravate or bring to a head the conflict between East and West.

The prospects depend, however, not only and not even primarily on what happens in the communist world. They may be determined more decisively by the trend of American policy.

Russia's new conciliatory attitude has been in the nature of a delayed reaction to the American policy of 'containing' communism, the policy of which George Kennan is widely regarded as the inspirer. Indeed the overtures of Malenkov's government are a signal success of that policy. The new Soviet leaders have acknowledged that the mutual pressure which East and West have brought to bear upon one another has resulted in an equilibrium which can form the basis for peace.

This indubitable success of the American policy of containment has, however, coincided with a crisis of that policy. Its inspirer has left the State Department at the very moment when official Washington might have celebrated him as the victor of the day. A cry to abandon 'containment' in favour of 'liberation', a cry to overthrow communist regimes in Eastern Europe and China, has gone up. Large sections of American opinion are clamouring for a crusade; and official Washington at times behaves as if it were anxious to yield to the clamour.

These auguries, when seen from Moscow, appear to promise little success for conciliatory overtures. Yet, Malenkov's government, not allowing itself to be discouraged, hopes to be able to calm the clamour for 'liberation', to dispel suspicion, and to induce the Western powers to revert to a policy 'based on facts'. But it also knows that if the West were in all earnestness to abandon 'containment' in favour of 'liberation', self-containment would become meaningless for the Soviet bloc.

Should a war-like threat come from the West before the new regime has had the time to consolidate itself, another dramatic shift may occur on the Russian scene: the Malenkov government may be compelled to withdraw and to make room for its opponents. It may be succeeded by a military dictatorship, a Soviet version of Bonapartism.

The dynamic potentialities of the Soviet State are still incalculable; and the emergence of a Soviet Bonaparte is one of the possible surprises. The part played by military leaders in the recent crisis in Moscow is still obscure in some respects, but there is no doubt that it was important.

The Russian revolution has been the only one among the modern revolutions which has so far not led to a military dictatorship. But the ghost of Bonaparte has haunted it for three decades; and both Trotsky and Stalin, each in his own way, wrestled with the ghost. Trotsky repeatedly warned the Bolshevik Party of the military dictator who one day might rise above its head and crush it. Stalin suspiciously scrutinized the faces of Tukhachevsky, Zhukov, and other marshals to see which of them might secretly nourish this dangerous ambition. As in Dante's tale about the man who wrestles with a snake and in the struggle himself assumes the snake's shape, Stalin assumed some features of a Soviet Bonaparte when, as Generalissimo, he placed himself above his generals. But this was in part a masquerade. Stalin remained the civilian party leader in uniform, representing only a diluted and adulterated Bonapartism.

The mere need for such an adulteration shows that the trend towards Bonapartism was latent in Soviet society; it was no mere invention of the lovers of historical analogy. The trend remained only latent, in part because Russia was until recently too weak to breed a Bonaparte. A Bonaparte cuts no figure if he cannot conquer a continent. The Soviet generals of the past were incapable of such a feat—Russia's industrial-military strength was altogether inadequate for that. At the close of the Stalin era this may no longer be true. Nobody can say whether a real general, whom the uniform of a Bonaparte would fit much better than it fitted Stalin, may not appear in the Red Square one day. It is not irrelevant to the situation in Russia that the trend towards the 'rule of the sword', to use an old-fashioned expression, has been so much at work in the non-communist world as well.

There are as yet no signs of the advent of a Soviet Bonaparte. But if the peace offers made by Stalin's civilian successors were to fail, it may be with him that the West will have to deal next.

The day on which a Russian Bonaparte rises in the Kremlin may see the end of all self-containment, for the Bonaparte would disperse the party secretaries and make straight for the English Channel.

CHAPTER TEN

FUTURE PROSPECTS:
DOMESTIC AFFAIRS

THE close interplay of domestic and foreign factors will determine the outlook of post-Stalin Russia. Just as an aggravation of the international situation may contribute to the emergence of a military dictatorship so domestic developments, in their turn, will exercise a powerful influence on foreign policy. It may, therefore, not be out of place to consider here the alternative directions in which the Soviet regime may evolve.

There are, broadly speaking, three possible variants of development:

(*a*) a relapse into the Stalinist form of dictatorship;
(*b*) a military dictatorship;
(*c*) a gradual evolution of the regime towards a socialist democracy.

The conditions under which each of these variants is likely to materialize deserve to be examined. An analysis of these conditions leads to the general conclusion that the balance of domestic factors favours a democratic regeneration of the regime. A *prolonged* relapse into Stalinism is highly improbable. The essential prerequisite for a military dictatorship would be a war-like threat from the West. The real alternative seems to lie therefore between military dictatorship and democratic evolution.

The great bourgeois revolutions, which were in a sense the predecessors of the Russian revolution, resulted in the establishment of military dictatorships. In Puritan

England and post-Jacobin France these dictatorships
came into being only a few years after the beginning of
the revolution. The Soviet regime is well advanced in its
fourth decade; but throughout this time it has preserved
its character as a civilian, not a military, dictatorship.

Before exploring further the prospects for the future,
we must briefly consider the main reason for this difference between the Russian and the other revolutions.

Every great revolution begins as a broad popular
movement, whose leaders strive to establish a system of
government very much more representative and broadly
based than that which prevailed under the old order.
Cromwell started by defending the rights of Parliament
against the Crown. The French revolution represented
at first all the Estates against the Court. The Russian
revolution sought to establish the rule of Councils of
Workers', Peasants', and Soldiers' Deputies in place of
Tsarist autocracy and the political vacuum of the
Kerensky regime.

Each revolution defeats the defenders of the old order,
because it enjoys massive popular support. But the end
of civil war brings about a state of weariness, frustration,
and political apathy. On the one hand, the new government loses popular support; on the other, society is incapable of governing itself. The old ruling classes are
destroyed or dispersed. The revolutionary classes are
exhausted, divided against themselves, confused, and
lacking in political energy and will. This was the state
of the middle classes in the English and French revolutions; and this was also the state of the Russian working
class in the early 1920's.

A disintegrated society, close to the brink of anarchy,
is incapable of producing a stable *and* representative
government, revolutionary or counter-revolutionary.
Since it is not in a position to govern itself, that is be
governed by its elected representatives, it of necessity
comes to be ruled by revolutionary 'usurpers'.

In such a disintegrated and politically amorphous

society power can be usurped and exercised only by an organization which, by its very nature or by force of tradition, has maintained a high degree of cohesion, discipline, and unity of will. In Puritan England and Thermidorian France only one such body existed: the army. The army was therefore predestined to act as trustee and guardian of post-revolutionary society. Cromwell was both the leader of the revolution and the commander of the Ironsides. In this double role he embodied both stages of the revolution: the representative—Parliamentary stage—and the later stage of the usurpatory Protectorate. In France there was a definite break between the two phases, and each was represented by different men. Bonaparte, who had played no significant role in the first phase, embodied the second.

The Russian revolution, too, developed from government by Soviet representation into a Protectorate by usurpation. But the Bolshevik Party, not the army, in this case provided that closely knit, disciplined body of men which, inspired by a single will, was capable of ruling and unifying the disintegrated nation. No such party had existed in previous revolutions. The Jacobin Party came into being only in the course of the upheaval. It was part of the fluctuating revolutionary tide; and it broke up and vanished at the ebb of the tide. The Bolshevik Party, on the other hand, had formed a solid and centralized organization long before 1917. This enabled it to make a revolution, to win a civil war, and then, after the ebb of the tide, to play the part the army had played elsewhere, and to secure by 'usurpation' the stability of the post-revolutionary government. The Bolsheviks alone were able to integrate forcibly the dislocated and splintered nation. It was they who created, inspired, and—what was more important—supervised the Red Army. Thus the same civilian body of men that had stood at the head of the revolution in the proletarian-democratic period, also acted as the dictatorial guardian of society throughout the protracted phase of unrepresentative government.

The party wielded the two main instruments of power, political police and army. It built up the political police into such a formidable instrument that it has had no need to call on the army to ensure stability of government. Nevertheless, the army has always been in the background as a potential counterbalance to the political police. The party has ensured its own predominance by keeping these twin instruments of power mutually in check. Each had an inherent tendency to make itself independent; but neither army nor police could assert its independence as long as the party was able to use one of them to suppress the other's appetite for power.

The quintessence of Stalin's mechanics of government consisted in balancing his regime on these two props. But the instruments of power do not operate in a vacuum. Their importance and effectiveness depends primarily on the nation's morale. The extent to which any regime relies for its stability on the use of force is in inverse proportion to the popular support it enjoys. Popular support, or its absence, is therefore the third and the decisive element in any mechanics of power.

Malenkov's government has struck a blow at the political police. If effective, the blow must cause a shift in the whole structure of the regime. One of its two props has been weakened, perhaps shattered. On the face of it, this upsets the equilibrium of the regime and tends to increase the importance of the other prop—the army. If the party has deprived itself of the ability to oppose the political police to the army, the army may become the decisive factor in domestic affairs. After a delay of several decades the Russian revolution may yet enter its Bonapartist phase.

However, such a development is possible only if the government does not enjoy enough popular support to make it relatively independent of the material instruments of power. Only if government by persuasion fails are the tools of coercion, their respective weight and mutual relation to one another, of decisive importance. A Bonaparte can reach out for power and have his 'r8th Brumaire' only in a country ruled by an ineffective Directory, where disorder is rampant, discontent rife, and the Directory is in frantic search of 'a good sword'. No army can set itself up as an independent political force against a government enjoying popular confidence. In domestic policy as in war the relation of morale to physical factors is as three to one.

From these general remarks on the mechanics of power we now pass to an examination of the three variants of development possible in Russia.

Relapse into Stalinism

An attempt by the political police to regain its former position cannot be ruled out. The decree of amnesty and the exposure of the 'doctors' plot' have been major moves in an intense struggle which is still in progress. As these lines are written a new indication of its scope becomes apparent. The former Minister of State Security in Soviet Georgia and several high officials of the Ministry have been arrested and charged with violation of constitutional rights of citizens and extortion of confessions. The local leaders of the party have been deposed for connivance.

The arrested Georgians have obviously been allies and subordinates of the die-hards of Stalinism defeated in Moscow. But the defeated faction has its allies and subordinates in each of the sixteen Soviet Republics. Each provincial capital has had its Ignatievs and Riumins who are now being removed from office, transferred to prison, and charged not as terrorists or spies, but as men guilty of violating the constitutional rights of citizens. Thus, the transition from one regime to another is being carried out by a series of moves amounting to rather more than a mere palace revolt and less than a real revolution.

In the 1930's Trotsky advocated a 'limited political revolution' against Stalinism. He saw it not as a fully fledged social upheaval but as an 'administrative operation' directed against the chiefs of the political police and a small clique terrorizing the nation. As so often, Trotsky was tragically ahead of his time and prophetic in his vision of the future, although he could not imagine that Stalin's closest associates would act in accordance with his scheme. What Malenkov's government is carrying out now is precisely the 'limited revolution' envisaged by Trotsky.

The die-hards of the security police may still try to rally and fight to save their skins. They may fight back from the provinces and they may try to regain the ground lost in Moscow. They may have influential associates and accomplices inside the Kremlin. They may try to remove Malenkov and his associates, denouncing them as apostates, secret Trotskyite-Bukharinites, and imperialist agents and presenting themselves as Stalin's only true and orthodox heirs.

Even if such a *coup* were successful, which is improbable, the restoration of Stalinism could be only a brief episode. The motives that caused men of Stalin's entourage to initiate a break with his era would continue to operate. Those motives spring from the present state and needs of the nation and are certainly shared by too many people to be defeated by the removal of a few personalities. Even if Malenkov were to be assassinated, others would fill his place. The political police is morally isolated. It has always been hated and feared. It is now hated more and feared less than ever. It has no chance of asserting itself against the combined strength of people, government, and party.

The diehards of the security police may, of course, join hands with the army. Signs of an ambiguous alliance between them and some military leaders were clearly visible in the incident of the Kremlin physicians in January 1953. But there have also been indications of a division among the army leaders. Not enough military support may therefore be available for a joint *coup*. But even if such a *coup* were to succeed, its result would be the establishment of a military dictatorship, not the restoration of the orthodox Stalinist regime. The prestige of the army stands high and is intact, while that of the police has been irreparably damaged. The police could be only the army's junior partner, and perhaps not even that—it might only be able to hold the stirrup for a Russian Bonaparte.

Military dictatorship

We have already mentioned the important part that some army leaders played in the political events of the last period. This emerges from the official, and now disavowed, statement about the plot of the Kremlin physicians, published on 13 January 1953. The statement contained the following curious passage:

'The criminal doctors tried *in the first instance to undermine the health of the leading Soviet military personnel, to put them out of action and thereby to weaken the country's defences.* They tried to put out of action Marshal A. M. Vassilevsky, Marshal L. A. Govorov, Marshal E. S. Koniev, General of the Army S. M. Shtemenko, Admiral G. E. Levchenko, and others. However, the arrest has upset the evil designs and the criminals have not succeeded in achieving their aim.' (My italics—I.D.)

The communiqué also claimed that the doctors had brought about the premature death of Zhdanov and Shcherbakov. Only these two *dead* party leaders figured as victims of the conspiracy. Not a single *living* party leader was mentioned as a prospective victim.

This omission was not accidental. Its significance becomes clear when this indictment is compared with accusations made in previous comparable cases. In every purge trial it was alleged that the 'terrorists' prepared to assassinate in the first instance the party leaders: Stalin, Molotov, Kaganovich, and others. The accusation levelled against the Kremlin doctors created a startlingly novel pattern. Not only did it not contain so much as a hint at a conspiracy against living civilian leaders—it stressed most emphatically that the 'conspirators' worked primarily or, rather, exclusively against the military.

After the official disavowal of the accusation, this last circumstance appears all the more significant. What—it must be asked—were the motives of the Ministry of State Security when it singled out military leaders as the sole targets of the imaginary conspiracy?

The Ministry clearly intended to build up the prestige of the marshals and generals and to play down the importance of party leaders. The assassination *motif* had a definite function in all the purge trials. It had been calculated to enhance the authority of the would-be victims of conspiracy. Prosecutor, judges, and Press had told the nation: 'These are our irreplaceable leaders. Their lives are most precious to our cause. Even the enemy knows this: and it is at them he aims. To their defence we ought to rally.' In the 'doctors' plot' the tale of assassination was intended to point the same moral. The Ministry of State Security was out to place the marshals and the generals on a pedestal and, by implication, to disparage the party leaders.[1]

Did the heads of the security police act on their own initiative when they accorded the marshals and generals the honour of being the only prospective victims of conspiracy? Or were perhaps some of the military chiefs not averse to being hailed as the nation's heroes and indispensable leaders? The security police had no special

[1] The Ministry may have aimed even further. The arrest of the doctors may have been intended as a preliminary to the arrest of Malenkov himself. The doctors were said to have speeded the death of Zhdanov. Since it was widely believed that Zhdanov had been Malenkov's rival, it would have been easy at the next stage to point to Malenkov as the chief instigator of the 'assassins'. But this is only a hypothesis. The special role of the military leaders in the whole affair is, however, not hypothetical, although certainly not all those mentioned in the communiqué are implicated.

reason to render this disinterested service to the marshals
and to exclude the party chiefs, unless it acted against the
latter with the complicity or on the instigation of the
former. The glory of martyrdom has more than once
enhanced a claim to power; and a bid for power was
implicit in the original story of the 'doctors' plot'. We
need not necessarily attribute personal political ambition
to any of the army leaders. They may have made an
initial move towards seizure of power from the conviction that it was their duty to frustrate the reforms and the
peace overtures contemplated by Malenkov. They may
have acted on the belief that the new policy will weaken
Russia militarily.

We have said that the tale about the 'doctors' plot',
the cry for vigilance, and the campaign against the Jews
were calculated to create an atmosphere of nationalist
and war-like hysteria, which would have ruled out the
possibility of any domestic reform and conciliatory
foreign policy. It should perhaps be added that the
extreme demonstrations of Russian nationalism have as
a rule been initiated or encouraged by the army, while
the party only connived at them willingly or reluctantly.
It was the army that fostered the cult of Kutuzov,
Suvorov, and the other traditional heroes of Russian
nationalism; and the army's influence was discernible in
the campaign against aliens, 'rootless cosmopolitans',
and other 'security risks'.

Between January and March 1953 a Russian Bonaparte
cast his shadow ahead. He has been compelled to withdraw. He may now be standing in the background and
watching the scene. Should Malenkov's government not
be able to master the situation, should discontent be rife,
should social discipline break down in consequence of
the reforms, and should danger from abroad coincide
with internal disorder, then the war-lord will step forward
again and seize power, with or without the aid of the
embittered die-hards of Stalinism.

A military dictatorship would signify neither a counter-revolution, in the Marxist sense, nor the restoration of Stalinism. Russia's military interest demands that the present economic order be conserved; and no military leader can or will do anything to change it fundamentally. His attitude towards the legacy of Bolshevism would hardly be very different from Napoleon's attitude towards the legacy of Jacobinism. He would not feel tied to any party tradition, and he would fill with his own martial splendour the vacuum left by the defunct Stalin cult. He, too, would be compelled to rationalize and modernize the system of government, but he would do so on a strictly authoritarian basis. If the internal tensions were to grow acute he would seek to relieve them by military adventure abroad. He might then out-Napoleon Napoleon and, before his own destruction, place Europe and Asia at Russia's feet.

Democratic regeneration

The prospect of a military dictatorship, while not altogether unreal, is improbable. The Russian people would have to prove extremely immature to exchange the rule of the *nagan* for the rule of the sword.[1] The present reaction against Stalinism indicates that the nation has outgrown authoritarian tutelage. Malenkov's reforms reflect a popular craving for freedom. To be sure, freedom may release discontent and lead to disorder and anarchy which would be a standing invitation to a new dictator. But freedom leads to such lamentable results only in nations too poor, or regimes too conservative, to satisfy the material needs of the people. In empty stomachs freedom turns sour. But Russia is no longer so poor and the regime is, after all, not so conservative. The economic progress made during the Stalin era has at last brought within the reach of the people a measure of well-being which should make possible an orderly winding-up of Stalinism and a gradual democratic evolution.

[1] *Nagan*—a revolver, originally of Belgian make, which was the standard weapon of the security police during a long period.

At the same time as Malenkov's government struck the blow at the security police it also decreed an overall reduction in the prices of most consumer goods. The reduction, ranging from 5 to 50 per cent, was the sixth consecutive measure of this kind carried out in the last three years. Since wages and salaries have either risen or remained stationary, the cumulative effect of the price cuts is a considerable rise in the standard of living. True enough, even the higher standard is far below the American and even below the Western European standard. But a comparison between national standards of living is largely irrelevant to the appreciation of Russia's morale.

To people rising from the lowest depth of poverty it matters little, if at all, that they enjoy none of the elaborate facilities and luxuries available to older industrial nations, that they have no motor-cars, refrigerators, vacuum cleaners, and washing machines, of the existence of which they often hardly know. They are aware that they are much better fed, clad, and shod than ever before; that the State provides their children with the most extensive facilities for education; and that the planned economy guarantees security of employment. They may also hope that, if there is no war, their vigorously expanding industry will soon bring within their reach the choicer goods and utilities as well. Under such conditions popular contentment is bound to grow; and so is popular confidence in a government which at last begins to fulfil the promise of a better life.

Fortified by this mood Malenkov's government evidently trusts in its ability to depart from the Stalinist regime without provoking dangerous unrest and exposing itself to effective counter-blows from its opponents.

Besides this positive reason the new rulers have a negative and less obvious reason for self-confidence.

Authoritarian governments initiating liberal reforms have often found that such reforms endangered their very existence, and have rapidly retraced their steps. But sometimes, although much more rarely, reform carried out in time disarmed popular resentment and strengthened the existing order. When resentment is deep, strong, and politically articulate an authoritarian government cannot save itself by reformist concessions. Each concession is seen as a sign of its weakness and encourages its irreconcilable opponents. Such, for instance, was the position of Nicholas II, the last Tsar. In 1905 he initiated an 'era of reform', but was compelled to bring it to an abrupt close. Towards the end of Tsardom all roads led to revolution: reform strengthened the hands of the revolutionaries; suppression intensified popular resentment and prepared the eventual explosion.

In contrast to this, the reforms decreed by Alexander II in 1855–61 isolated the radical opponents of Tsardom and made revolution impossible for half a century. Social discontent had been strong enough to demand reform; but it was not widespread and articulate enough to use the government's concessions as the starting-point for an all-out onslaught. Revolutionaries who, in the reign of Alexander II, went to the peasants to tell them that the Tsar had cheated them, were manhandled by the peasants and taken to the nearest police station.

The position of Malenkov's government is more like that of Alexander II than like that of Nicholas II. The political muteness of the nation at the end of the Stalin era is an asset to Stalin's successors. So little had the people expected a change and so little had they been capable of achieving it that they would have been exhilarated even by the most modest reforms—and Malenkov's reforms are by no means so modest. The contrast between the state of affairs of April 1953 and that of April 1952 already speaks more loudly in favour of the new rulers than they speak themselves. Anyone lifting his hand against the government would come under a cloud of popular suspicion as one who interferes with the salutary change. The people's patience and hopefulness may secure the stability of Malenkov's government and the chance of a gradual democratic regeneration of the regime.

What is to be understood by this 'democratic regeneration'?

Its beginning consists in the abolition of the practice of government under which all authority and power of decision were vested in a single leader. This practice characterized the working of the Stalinist administration from top to bottom. The autocrat in the Kremlin had his replicas on every level in government and party. The district party secretary or the chief of a provincial administration was as little subject to control from below and as arbitrary in the exercise of power as was Stalin himself. In recent years the party repeatedly tried to put an end to this state of affairs but in vain. The officials below danced to the tune played on the first fiddle in the Kremlin. As long as autocracy was untamed and unrestricted at the very top of government, arbitrary power lower down defied all attempts to tame it.

This has begun to change. Contrary to expectation, Malenkov has not 'stepped into Stalin's shoes'. At the top, government by committee has taken the place of government by a single leader. The Council of Ministers and the Central Committee, not Malenkov, speak on behalf of government and party. Thus a practice which prevailed in the Leninist period is, up to a point, restored.

The change-over has been made easier by the fact that even under Stalin the *Führerprinzip* never became the party's precept. It was practised in defiance of the accepted theory, not in accordance with it. Despite the Stalin cult, the notions of '*democratic* centralism' were instilled in the mind of the party insistently enough to make it possible for Stalin's successors to break with the autocratic principle, without necessarily appearing to depart from Stalinism. It used to be said of the Inquisition that it undid itself because even while it tortured infidels and heretics in the most un-Christian manner it continued to preach the Gospel and to teach the faithful to 'love thy neighbour'. Similarly, Stalinism has contributed to its own undoing by preaching the proletarian-democratic gospel of Leninism.

Government by committee necessitates free discussion, at least within the committee. The call for free discussion in the party often resounded during Stalin's last years, and it was addressed by the leaders of the party to the rank and file. But nobody could take the call seriously and act on it as long as there was no sign of free discussion higher up, and as long as the dreaded agents of the security police listened in. Now, at last, the call has a more genuine and convincing ring.

Yet for a nation and a party intimidated and gagged during decades nothing may be so difficult as the recovery of speech. Free discussion? But what is there to be discussed? How is a beginning to be made? Who is to start discussion and on what issue? And if repression returns, what will happen to those who opened their mouths? Uncertainty, embarrassment, and awkward silence are the first answer to appeals for free discussion.

One can gauge this mood even from the Soviet Press. The writers have been told that they need not go on mumbling the old magic formulæ, and that they ought to deal more freely with events and ideas. Tired as they must be of the old formulæ, they are lost without them; and they do not know what to say.

Once again the example must be set by the new rulers. They themselves must begin to discuss affairs of State publicly. But they are naturally afraid of doing so. If they begin to air their differences at this early stage, they will give the impression of disunity and weakness. They prefer to settle their inevitable disagreements within their own narrow circle, and to demonstrate to the country and the world that they are inspired by a single will. Nor does their ambiguous attitude towards Stalinist orthodoxy allow them frankly to explain the direction of their policy, or even to see it clearly for themselves.

But sooner or later they must set the example. Either their own differences will become wide and acute enough to compel some of them to appeal for support to public opinion, or else the rank and file, constantly exhorted to use their democratic rights, will begin to speak after an interval of perplexity and silence; and the discussion down below may become chaotic and anarchic, unless guidance is offered from above.

The process by which the nation may relearn to form and express its opinions may at first be slow and difficult. It can start only from inside the Communist Party. The regime will, either from self-preservation or from inertia, continue as a single party system for years to come. This need not be an important obstacle to democratic evolution as long as party members are permitted to speak their minds on all matters of policy. All politically minded and active elements of the nation are, anyhow, in the ranks of the Communist Party, if only because there has been no other party to turn to. And within the Communist Party there already exist various potential trends which will become actual and will crystallize in the processes of inner party discussion. Diverse shades of internationalism and nationalism will come to life. Divergent attitudes towards the peasantry will be expressed. Conflicting views will arise about the tempo of further industrialization, consumer interests, educational issues, and a host of other vital problems.

Once the ruling party begins to discuss its affairs it cannot monopolize freedom of discussion for long. It cannot forbid members of other organizations—trade unions, collective farms, co-operatives, Soviets, and educational associations—to do what its own members are allowed and encouraged to do.

The coming epoch may thus bring with it a breathtaking reversal of the process by which the Soviet democracy of the early days of the revolution was transformed into an autocracy.

The Leninist regime did not begin as a single party

system. On the contrary, its first promise, made in good faith, was that it would treat with tolerance all parties which did not oppose the revolution arms in hand—for all those parties there was to be room within the new Soviet democracy. Fighting for the life of the revolution and for its own life, Lenin's government broke that promise. It destroyed Soviet democracy and banned all parties; but it still preserved democracy within Bolshevik ranks. Yet it could not allow the Bolsheviks the freedom which it had denied to others. Lenin proceeded to restrict inner party democracy, and Stalin abolished it.

The reverse process can begin only with the infusion of democracy in the Communist Party. Only from there can freedom of expression spread to other bodies, covering an ever wider range, until a fully fledged Soviet democracy comes into being, backed by a high industrial civilization and by an up-to-date socialist system.

Historically, the Communist Party has lost its own freedom because it denied it to others. When at last it regains freedom it cannot but return it to others.

This great goal still looms only dimly on a distant horizon. To come nearer to it, Russia needs peace, peace, and once again peace. However half-hearted the intentions of the Malenkov government may have been and whatever its ultimate fate, it already has the historic distinction that it has taken the first steps which should lead towards democratic regeneration.

For decades freedom was banned from Russia because it was, or was supposed to be, the enemy of socialism. If Russia had been free to choose her own road she would hardly have marched in the direction in which Bolshevism has led her. But freedom may once again become the ally and friend of socialism; and then the forty years of wandering in the desert may be over for the Russian revolution.

POSTSCRIPT

THE BERIA AFFAIR

BERIA'S downfall, announced on 10 July, marks the end of a distinct phase in Russia's political evolution after Stalin.

During that phase, which lasted from March till the end of June, the advocates of reform at home and conciliation abroad were on the ascendant, while the diehards of Stalinism and the 'anti-appeasers' were compelled to yield one position after another.

The East German revolt of 16 and 17 June brought into play a new factor which discomfited the reformers and conciliators and allowed their opponents to strike a counter-blow, the first since Stalin's death. Inside the ruling group a coalition of the most diverse groups and interests raised the cry: 'Enough of "liberalism"! Enough of appeasement! Enough of the betrayal of Stalinist orthodoxy!' To the world's amazement, Beria, Stalin's countryman, henchman, admiring biographer, and for many years chief policeman, was denounced as the arch-traducer of Stalinism.

The Beria affair is undoubtedly an incident in the personal rivalry between Stalin's successors. It represents one stage in the process by which a candidate for the vacant post of the autocrat may strive to eliminate his competitors. But personal rivalry is only one of the elements of the drama: and in itself it is of secondary importance. More significant is the conflict of principles and policies hidden behind the clash of personalities—the world is interested in the policies rather than the personalities which are going to emerge victorious.

175

Let us briefly survey the trend of Soviet policies since Stalin's death in order to see which are the major issues at stake.

From March to the middle of June one domestic reform followed upon another in close succession. The Stalin cult was virtually abolished. A campaign of 'enlightenment' was in progress, designed to make it impossible to replace that cult by the adulation of any other Leader. The administration was being overhauled and shaken from its Byzantine-totalitarian rigidity. A fairly comprehensive amnesty was decreed. The frame-up of the Kremlin doctors was declared null and void. The inquisitorial methods of the political police were bluntly condemned. The rule of law was proclaimed. Strong emphasis was placed on the constitutional rights of the citizen. Newspapers asked almost openly for the abolition of censorship and official control. (*The Literary Gazette*, for instance, frankly demanded that the Soviet theatre be allowed to manage its own affairs without outside interference, a demand which nobody would have dared to raise during the Stalin era and which obviously set an infectious example to others.) The need for the 'monolithic' outlook was implicitly or even explicitly questioned at almost every step. Free expression of views was encouraged; and the holder of unorthodox views was no longer labelled an enemy, a traitor, or a foreign agent. High officials were demoted merely on the ground that they abused their power and acted unconstitutionally; no predatory or counter-revolutionary intent was attributed to them. The relaxation of the over-centralistic method of government was noticeable above all in the dismissal of Russifiers from high office in the Ukraine, in Georgia, and other outlying Union Republics. Russification was emphatically disavowed. Together with the cessation of anti-Semitic incitement these moves promised a new and hopeful beginning in the treatment of the smaller nationalities.

Last but not least, the government ordered a revision

of the targets of the current economic plans. Consumer industries were to raise their output. A higher standard of living and contentment of the masses were obviously regarded as vital preconditions for the success of the new policy.

A new spirit made itself felt in the conduct of foreign affairs. Moscow consistently exercised its influence in favour of a truce in Korea; and not even Synghman Rhee's provocations diverted the Russians (or the Chinese or the North Koreans) from this path. In Europe Malenkov's government began, as it was forecast, 'to explore the lines of retreat from Germany'.[1]

It is enough to recall here the moves made by Soviet diplomacy only during the week which preceded the Berlin revolts:

After General Chuikov had been recalled from Berlin the whole policy of the Pieck-Ulbricht government was dramatically reversed. The 'iron curtain' between Eastern and Western Germany was nearly demolished. Labour policy was revised. The struggle between the government and the Evangelical Church was called off; and the Church regained its former privileges. Collectivization of farming was stopped. The farmers who had fled to Western Germany were invited to come back and take possession of their property. Private capital was also invited to return to industry and trade.

From the Russian viewpoint these moves made no sense at all unless they were part and parcel of a policy calculated to bring about the unification of Germany and the withdrawal of occupation armies. There was little doubt in Berlin that Moscow was really prepared to abandon the government of Pieck and Ulbricht. So strongly indeed did Soviet representatives in Berlin encourage this belief and so frankly did they negotiate with non-Communist leaders about a change of the regime that by this alone the Russians themselves unwittingly induced the people of Berlin to descend upon

[1] See above, p. 153.

M

the streets, to clamour for the resignation of the Communist government, and to storm that government's offices. 'Russia is willing to abandon her puppets—let us remove them at once!' this was the idea behind the German revolt.

In the same week, on 10 June, Moscow established diplomatic relations with Austria and proclaimed an end to the regime of occupation there. Restrictions on inter-zonal traffic were abolished in Austria as well. And on the same day, as a side-line, Moscow solemnly renounced all its claims on Turkey, the claims that had played a fateful role in the opening phases of the cold war.

What was surprising in all these developments, domestic and foreign, was their extraordinary consistency and apparently frictionless progress. Stalin's successors showed no sign of hesitation in pursuing the new course. They betrayed no second thoughts. They seemed to bask in the glory of unaccustomed generosity.

Was it possible, one wondered, that the die-hards of Stalinism and other opponents of 'appeasement' should be so weak and discredited that they were unable to put a brake upon the new course? Or were they perhaps retreating tactically and merely waiting until the new policy had run into serious trouble?

Where did Beria stand in all this? To which faction did he belong?

In watching the Russian scene it is not difficult to arrive, by processes of deduction and analysis, at a definition of the broad viewpoints and political conceptions contending for acceptance by the ruling group. Nor is it very difficult to see the sectional interests and aspirations reflected in the competing conceptions. The broad forces aligned with, or arrayed against, one another throw their shadows sharply enough even across the veil of secrecy that surrounds them for the outsider to be able to guess the approximate disposition of those forces. But only in exceptional cases is it possible to venture even a guess about the attitude of this or that official personality on any specific issue.

In *Russia After Stalin* the supposition was expressed that 'in the inner councils of the party Beria did not necessarily represent the anti-liberal attitude of the police', that he may, on the contrary, have acted against the 'die-hards of the police' as one of the promoters of reform.

This supposition appears to have been borne out by the facts in the meantime. In the last period of his activity Beria represented the curious paradox of a semi-liberal police chief in a totalitarian state. The period up to the East German revolt might indeed be described as Beria's Hundred Days.

Beria took upon himself the responsibility for two major political acts, two unforgivable 'crimes' in the eyes of the die-hards of Stalinism and their associates. First, he humiliated the political police when he exposed its practices in connection with the 'doctors' plot'. Next, he offended, 'Great Russian chauvinism' when he, the Georgian, called for an end to Russification in Georgia, in the Ukraine, in the Baltic lands, and in Central Asia.

Both these acts, the former more explicitly than the latter, had ostensibly been endorsed by the other party leaders. But as Minister of the Interior Beria was identified with these acts more closely than anyone else. No wonder that some of the old hands of the political police, resentfully straining to recover their sacred right to extort 'confessions' from their victims, and the Great Russian chauvinists, joined hands to wreak vengeance on him.

Beria was less directly associated with the conduct of foreign affairs; but, as a member of the Politbureau (now the Praesidium), he exercized a strong influence in that field, too. Bolshevik foreign policy has never been made by the Foreign Minister of the day, Molotov, Vyshinsky, Litvinov, or Chicherin—it has always been the prerogative of the Politbureau. That foreign and domestic policies are closely interdependent has been an axiom. The man in charge of domestic security must therefore have had a considerable say in foreign affairs as well. Beria certainly had a decisive say in the affairs of Eastern Germany and generally of Eastern Europe, which had a direct bearing on Russia's internal security, on the one hand, and on diplomacy, on the other. Thus his opponents could easily blame him for 'appeasement' as well as for the domestic reforms.

From March to June Beria acted in close alliance with Malenkov. Together they swayed the Praesidium, probably against Molotov's and certainly against Khrushchev's opposition or semi-opposition. Jointly they represented the strongest bloc of power within the Praesidium. The new policy aroused great hopes and was undoubtedly very popular; and as long as this was so, nobody could challenge Malenkov's and Beria's joint authority.

(Against this interpretation the old argument may be advanced that under a totalitarian regime the states of the popular mind and the social, cultural and moral trends at work in society are of no political importance. In his criticism of *Russia After Stalin*, Mr. George F. Kennan, for instance, writes that the 'majority of students of modern totalitarianism . . . feel that *if the ruling group remains united, vigilant* and ruthless, it need not defer extensively to, or be seriously influenced by, subjective feelings within the populace at large'. And again: 'In general, totalitarian leaders *who retain their internal unity* and their ruthlessness can scoff at subjective states of the popular mind. . . .' (My italics—I.D.)

Mr. Kennan's words, written before Beria's fall, reflected an assumption that there was no need for Western policy to take into account any genuine divisions within the Soviet ruling group, because no such

divisions existed. This assumption has been proved
wrong. But what conclusion is to be drawn from the fact
that the Soviet ruling group does not 'remain united'
and does not 'retain its internal unity'? Surely the
'subjective states of the popular mind' do acquire some
political significance thereby? And those states of mind
may in part even account for the differences within the
ruling group itself?)

From the beginning, however, the forces opposed to
the Malenkov-Beria policy were formidable. The old
hands of the political police were not idle. Some party
stalwarts were shocked by the all round break with the
old-established canons of Stalinism. Some chiefs of
armed forces pondered with alarm the implications of
the quasi-liberal reforms: Would the reforms not cause
a slump in labour discipline and imperil the armament
programmes? By dint of tradition the army has been
the mouthpiece of 'Great Russian chauvinism' and has
viewed with suspicion and hostility the 'centrifugal'
nationalisms of the outlying Republics. Some marshals
and generals could not adopt a favourable attitude towards a foreign policy obviously directed towards an
eventual withdrawal of the occupation armies from
Germany and Austria.

But the coalition of shocked Stalinist diehards,
resentful policemen, and anxious generals was helpless
as long as the new policy was triumphantly carried forward on a tide of popular enthusiasm. The first hitches
apparently occurred on the home front. To judge from
circumstantial evidence, labour discipline did slump in
industry, and collective farms lagged with food deliveries.
But these hitches were either not serious enough to permit the opponents of the new policy to launch a frontal
attack on it, or else they did not provide convenient
ground for such an attack.

It was Eastern Germany that gave the opponents of
the new policy the opportunity they had eagerly awaited.

The Germans who on 16 and 17 June descended upon

the streets, clamouring for the dismissal of the government of Pieck and Ulbricht, assailing the People's Police, and meeting Russian tanks with a hail of stones, did in fact bring about an upheaval; but the upheaval took place in Moscow, not in Berlin.

Almost certainly a cry against 'appeasement' went up at once within the walls of the Kremlin. Army chiefs could now argue that it was the army that had to bear the consequences of the neck-breaking political experiments started by the civilians; that order reigned in Eastern Germany as long as General Chuikov ruled there with an iron hand; that the trouble began as soon as the general had been replaced by Semyonov, as High Commissioner, and a civilian regime had been established; and that then it was the army that had to rescue that regime.

Starting from the German issue the critics could turn against the new policy as a whole. They could point out that not only Germany but the West at large was receiving Russian concessions as proof of Russian weakness; and that Washington in particular was using these concessions as the starting point for an intensified onslaught on Russia's positions in Eastern and Central Europe.

Moreover, the ruling group saw that the new policy was indeed becoming a source of weakness for Russia: it plunged the whole of Eastern Europe into a turmoil; it caused a rapid deterioration in Russia's bargaining position; it tempted American diplomacy to pass from 'containment' to 'liberation'; and it threatened to rob Russia of the fruits of her victory in the Second World War, without any compensating gains.

The 'appeasers' may still have argued that the new line had not yet been given a chance; that it would be wrong to abandon it immediately after it had encountered the first difficulties; and that only by persisting patiently in the policy of concessions could the Soviet Government reap its benefits.

But after the earthquake in Eastern Germany, after
the tremors in Hungary and Czechoslovakia, after all
the calls for a tough policy which resounded from
Washington, the argument against 'appeasement' carried more weight in the Kremlin.

In Russia as in the United States there exist groups
which hold the view that all peace-seeking is futile;
these groups regard with *Schadenfreude* any setback
suffered by the conciliators. The position of such groups
was now greatly enhanced: the advocates of a tough
policy in the West had effectively played into their hands.

There is no reason, however, to assume that after 16
and 17 June these extremists became the real masters
of Soviet policy. The core of the ruling group still consists of men prepared to seek agreement with the West.
But even the men of the 'centre' must have been affected
by the arguments against 'appeasement'. They had to
admit that the conduct of Soviet policy since Stalin's
death was rather inept in some respects.

They had to admit that Moscow was over-hasty in
making concessions and over-zealous in demonstrating
its willingness to make further and more far-reaching
concessions. Official spokesmen had many times confi-
dently stated that the government would never accept
Washington's demand that Russia must yield substantial
ground before the West opened negotiations. In fact
Malenkov's government behaved as if it had tacitly
accepted that demand—it did make concessions in
advance of negotiations.

Even from the viewpoint of the Soviet appeaser the
initiation of the mild course in Eastern Germany turned
out to have been 'premature'. It provoked a near collapse
of the Communist regime there.

From the Soviet viewpoint it would have been justifi-
able to take such risks only after the West had agreed
to an all-round withdrawal of the occupation armies.
The undoing of the Communist regime in Eastern
Germany would then be the price Russia paid for a

German settlement and a stop to the armament race. But to start paying this price so early in the game was the peak of folly, from the Kremlin's viewpoint.

Thus even the men of the 'centre', who had hitherto backed the new policy, had to recognize the need for a change in tone and perhaps in tactics, even if they were not at all inclined to give up the quest for 'peaceful coexistence'. Finding themselves under deadly fire from the extreme groups, they were all too anxious to disclaim responsibility for the 'appeasement' of recent months, and to throw the blame for it on someone else.

The East German revolt also provided an opening for an attack on domestic reform. To be sure, not all the adherents of conciliation abroad stood also for reform at home; and not all the reformers need have been appeasers. Nevertheless, there exists a broad correspondence between the two aspects of policy; and amid the tension created by the events in Germany both aspects became vulnerable.

The sense of security and the optimism which had characterized Russia's mood in the spring had gone. The cry for vigilance resounded anew and with fresh vigour. Soldier, policeman and Stalinist stalwart could point accusing fingers at the advocates of reform:

Your policy, so they could say, has already brought disaster in Berlin and caused dangerous trouble in Budapest and Prague. Soon it may bring disaster nearer home. In Moscow the people are already whispering about an impending depreciation of the rouble, and the Minister of Finance was compelled to speak about this in public. Discipline is becoming slack in the factories. Trouble is brewing in the collective farms. The newspapers in their newfangled zeal for free criticism are sapping popular respect for authority. If you are allowed to continue this policy, you will bring about a 16 June here in Moscow!

The phantom of a 16 June in Moscow struck fear into the hearts of the reformers and paralysed their wills.

In Chapter X, three possible variants of developments were discussed: (*a*) democratic regeneration; (*b*) a relapse into Stalinism; and (*c*) a military dictatorship. It was pointed out that the prerequisite for a military dictatorship would be a war-like threat to Russia from the West.

The picture of events is in fact more confused and contradictory than the theoretical forecast. *Grau is jede Theorie, ewig grün ist des Lebens Baum.* Yet the theoretical analysis still provides the clue to the picture.

The East German events, followed by the call to revolt addressed to Eastern Europe from the West, presented Moscow with a substitute for a 'war-like threat', with half such a threat. This was not enough to bring about a military coup. But it was quite enough to bring back into action that coalition of groups in army and police which had shown its hand in the affair of the Kremlin doctors in January. Roughly the same combination of cliques which had concocted the doctors' plot carried out a semi-coup against the reformers and 'appeasers' after 16 and 17 June.

Under this attack the alliance between Malenkov and Beria broke down. The attack was evidently powerful enough to make Malenkov feel that he could save his own position only by shifting his ground and throwing Beria to the lions. And Malenkov succeeded indeed in saving his position.

'The diehards of the security police may still try to rally and fight to save their skins. [These words were written in the middle of April[1]]. They may fight back from the provinces and they may try to regain the ground lost in Moscow. They may have influential associates and accomplices inside the Kremlin. They may try to remove Malenkov and his associates, denouncing them as apostates, secret Trotskyite-Bukharinites, and imperialist agents, and presenting themselves as Stalin's only true and orthodox heirs.'

[1] See above, p. 164.

This has come true, only that so far Beria, not Malenkov, has been 'removed' and 'denounced as apostate'; and Malenkov has sought to insure his position by consenting to play the part of Beria's chief denouncer.

Beria was in a peculiarly vulnerable position. His name had been associated with the darkest aspects of Stalinism in the last fifteen years, with concentration camps, mass deportations, and thought control; with the iron curtain; and with the purge trials in the satellite countries. He had performed all the unsavoury jobs assigned to him by Stalin. Yet after his master's death he unmasked himself as a *dvurushnik* and a 'liberal' at heart. His own police despised him as a 'liberal'; and the people hated him as the chief of the police. His head, the head which belonged to the 'most powerful and most dreaded man of Russia', was therefore the easiest prize to win for the opponents of reform. Both the police and the people almost certainly rejoiced at his downfall. The people believed that only now would the era of freedom begin for good, while the diehards of the political police were confident that only now did the crazy spring of liberal reform come to an end.

On the face of it, the fall of Beria might be seen as a necessary stage in Russia's democratic evolution; and thus Malenkov has vaguely presented it. The chief accusation he levelled against Beria was that Beria had conspired to place the political police above party and government and thus to block the road of reform. Beria, so Malenkov stated, carried out the recent reforms only because he had to: these reforms having been decided on the joint initiative of the Central Committee and the Praesidium, Beria pretended to carry them out loyally, while in fact he obstructed their execution. As if to confirm this version, the Central Committee restated its criticism of the Stalin cult, its opposition to the adulation of any Leader, and its determination to secure 'collective leadership', free debate, and the rule of law.

If this were all, one might indeed see the downfall of Beria as a further stage in Russia's revulsion against Stalinism. But this is not all.

What is ominous in this grim affair is, of course, not Beria's downfall but the manner in which it was brought about. He was denounced as a traitor and enemy of the party and the people, and as an agent of foreign imperialism who aimed at the restoration of capitalism. This is the 'classical' 'amalgam' of the Stalinist purges of the 1930's. Thus, the re-enactment of the Witches' Sabbath, which failed to come off in January, appears to have begun after all, with Beria, instead of the Kremlin doctors, hovering 'through the fog and filthy air'.

The reproduction of the 'amalgam' of the 1930's makes a mockery of the claim of the ruling group that it defended the principle of collective leadership against Beria. That principle implies unhampered expression of political differences within the leading group and ultimately within the party as a whole. But who will dare to speak his mind freely when he has reason to fear that for this he may be denounced as traitor and foreign agent? The Stalinist amalgam rules out free discussion and consequently 'collective leadership'.

If it was possible to see a promise of democratic regeneration in Russia after Stalin's death, this was so in part because denunciations of this sort had disappeared—they had become rare even during Stalin's last years. The many high officials demoted between March and June were not labelled foreign agents, spies, or adherents of capitalism. They were charged with concocting false accusations, abusing power, imposing policies of Russification, and so on. These were plausible charges, self-explanatory within a certain political context, and fitting in with the circumstances in which the dismissed men, whether guilty or not, had operated. The charges were made in a moderate and sober language in which there was no hint of a witch hunt.

In contrast to this, the accusations levelled against

Beria were full of irrational, demonological overtones; and the world was asked to believe that the man who had been in charge of Russia's domestic security during the Second World War was an agent of foreign imperialism.

The meaning of the Beria affair emerges even more conclusively from the fact that his fall became the signal for a new drive against the 'nationalisms' of the Georgians, Ukrainians, and other non-Russian nationalities. It was no sheer coincidence that during the 'liberal spring' Great Russian chauvinism was kept in check and the need was proclaimed to give more scope to the aspirations and demands of the non-Russian Republics.

Policy towards the smaller nations is the most sensitive barometer of the general atmosphere of the Soviet Union. Liberalization means less central control and more autonomy for non-Russians. Police rule implies strict centralization; and its tightening usually leads to a drive against the 'bourgeois' nationalisms of the outlying Republics.

Between March and June the talk was, characteristically, against operating the bogy of '*alleged* bourgeois nationalisms' in the non-Russian provinces. In what seemed a long overdue act of historical justice the Russifiers were dismissed from office in Tiflis and Kiev.

It should perhaps be recalled that the Stalin era began precisely with a struggle against the 'nationalist deviationists' in Georgia and the Ukraine. It was on this subject that Lenin, mortally ill, wrote his last, great, angry, and stirring letter to the party. (The author has read the full text of this letter which has remained unpublished till this day.) In it Lenin expressed the sense of shame and even of personal guilt which Stalin's drive against the 'nationalist deviationists' had aroused in him. He warned the party against the Great Russian chauvinism of the Soviet bureaucracy and of Stalin in particular, against the barbarous violence of that 'truly Russian Great Bully', who, evoking the need for strict central government, would oppress, insult, and humiliate the non-Russian nationalities. Lenin passionately argued that it would be a thousand times better for the Soviet Republic even to forgo somead vantages of centralized government than 'to deliver the smaller nationalities into the hands of the Great Russian Bully'.

There was therefore a curious historical symmetry in the circumstance that immediately after Stalin's death the Georgian and Ukrainian issues reappeared on the agenda and that this time an attempt was made to tame the 'truly Russian Great Bully'.

But the Great Bully seems to have come back to bait the 'bourgeois nationalists' of Georgia and the Ukraine; and his return is the surest sign of some reaction against the progressive reforms of preceding months.

Under the pretext of frustrating Beria's ambition to secure the predominance of the political police, an attempt seems in fact to be made to re-establish that predomin- ance.

The struggle is still on, however, and its outcome has hardly been decided. The diehards of Stalinism have scored only half a victory.

In some respects the Beria affair is unique and cannot even be compared with any of Stalin's great purges.

None of Stalin's victims wielded, on the eve of a purge, power comparable to Beria's; and none had such a following within the bureaucracy. Stalin finally destroyed Bukharin, Zinoviev, Kamenev, and their like after having first patiently, slyly, and in the course of many years deprived them of the last shred of power, discredited them, and rendered them harmless. On the eve of his trial Tukhachevsky was powerful enough as a military personality; but he had no political standing. Yagoda was a mere executor of Stalin's will. In 1936–38 Stalin had already his hands firmly on all levers of power and nobody dared to challenge his autocratic position.

Not so Malenkov. He has apparently embarked upon the slippery road of purges even before he stands on his own feet. His leadership is not yet acknowledged. His position of power is not yet consolidated. He must still speak and act as one of a team. The party is 'rallying' not behind 'Comrade Malenkov' but 'around the Central Committee'. Malenkov's position today is not appreciably stronger than Beria's was yesterday.

If it was possible to overthrow Beria so easily, what guarantee is there that Malenkov cannot be disgraced with just as little effort? If party meetings could be so rapidly persuaded to acclaim the fall of one triumvir, may they not look upon the destruction of any other triumvir with equal indifference?

The fate of Stalin's successors may yet prove less similar to that of Stalin than to that of Danton, Desmoulins, and Robespierre, who sent each other to the guillotine, while none of them enjoyed exclusive authority, with the result that all were destroyed. It is, of course, also possible that after a series of purge trials Malenkov may finally emerge as the new autocrat; but this is by no means certain.

The divisions in the ruling group reflect in the last instance conflicting pressures exerted upon it by outside forces which in the long run work either towards a military dictatorship or towards democratic regeneration. The Beria affair represents therefore only one moment in the kaleidoscopic movement of contemporary Russian history.

The army chiefs no longer watch the scene in passivity and silence. Their influence was clearly discernible in the affair of the Kremlin doctors. It was even more distinct in the Beria affair. Without the army's assured support Malenkov would not have dared to strike at Beria, who nominally still had the whole body of the political police under his orders, and who at any rate could still rely on some section of the police to rally to his defence. It was no matter of chance that Moscow's Press and radio gave so much prominence to the speeches against Beria made by Marshals Zhukov,

Vassilevsky, Sokolovsky, Govorov, and others. During the great Stalinist purges the leaders of the officers' corps did not appear so conspicuously on the political stage. Even so, Stalin felt his position to be threatened by Tukhachevsky. How much more may Malenkov's position be imperilled by his Marshals, whose military glory and popular appeal are far superior to Tukhachevsky's.

'Malenkov's government has struck a blow at the political police! [It was pointed out in Chapter X]. If effective the blow must cause a shift in the whole structure of the regime. One of its two props has been weakened, perhaps shattered. On the face of it, this upsets the equilibrium of the regime and tends to increase the importance of the other prop—the army. If the party has deprived itself of the ability to oppose the political policy to the army, the army may become the decisive factor in domestic affairs.'

Paradoxically, the regime now seems to make an attempt to repair that shattered prop, the political police, with the army's help. But for some time to come, until the Beria faction is completely eliminated, the political police will remain in a state of disarray, robbed of its normal striking power; more than ever the government will have to rely for its internal security on the army. It must take some time before the structure of power characteristic of Stalinism is restored, if it can be restored at all. Until then a gap will yawn between the galvanized Stalinist method of government and theun-Stalinist mechanics of power. Across this gap a potential Bonaparte once again casts his shadow.

Nor have the forces vanished which drove the ruling group to decree the reforms of last spring, although at the moment, they may have suffered a severe setback. The reforms could not have sprung merely from Beria's, or from anybody else's, whim and ambition. They met a need felt deeply and widely by the nation. Malenkov and his associates still pay a tribute to the popular mood when they go on declaring that they intend to pursue the course initiated after Stalin's death. The popular mood compels them to tread a twisted path rather cautiously, and it may even compel them to keep part of their promise.

Moreover, the recent reforms corresponded to Russia's new social structure and outlook which, although formed during the Stalin era, have become incompatible with Stalinism.

No shift within the ruling group, no court intrigue, no coup or counter-coup, and not even bloody purges can obliterate these basic factors, which continue to operate against the inertia of Stalinism. If they are not destroyed by a new world war, and if they are not unduly cramped by fear of war, the popular mood and the urges of society will sooner or later force open the road of reform once again. And then they will keep it open more firmly than they did in the liberal spring of 1953.

15 July 1953

DK274 .D43   CU-Main
c.1
Deutscher, Isaac, 1/Russia after Stalin; with a po

3 9371 00033 8418